A Confession ------

We repent and earnestly request your forgiveness
for all we have left undone.

For our insensitivity to the needs of others, that
prevent us from giving generously to them.

For our prejudice and fear of others, that prevents
us from loving them.

For our resentment of others, that prevents us from
forgiving them.

For our impatience with others, that prevents us
from understanding them.

For our neglectfulness of others, that prevents
us from using our particular gifts for them.

And finally for our pride and selfishness that
excludes your Holy Spirit from our own spirit
and from ourselves.

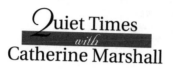

Quiet Times
with
Catherine Marshall

Quiet Times *with* Catherine Marshall

Second Edition

Catherine Marshall

and Leonard LeSourd

Chosen Books

A Division of Baker Book House Co
Grand Rapids, Michigan 49516

Published by Chosen Books
a division of Baker Book House Company
P.O. Box 6287, Grand Rapids, MI 49516-6287

Revised edition of *Personal Prayer Journal,* published in 1988. *Personal Prayer Journal* was published previously as *My Personal Prayer Diary* in 1979.

Printed in the United States of America

ISBN 0-8007-9248-3

Contents

Acknowledgments   7

One Hour, a Bible, and an Open Mind   8
How This Book Can Help You Grow Spiritually   12
How to Use This Book   17
Quiet Times with Catherine Marshall   19

Topical Index   235

Acknowledgments

We are indebted to Alice Watkins for her research into prayer books and various Bible translations and for tirelessly typing and retyping the prayers as we revised them; to Edith Marshall for her research and helpful contributions. We also wish to thank Page Bailey, Betty Schneider, and Louise Gibbons of the Chosen Books staff for prayer suggestions and typing help. Also to Jeanne Sevigny for typing help and suggestions for the revised edition. And to Patricia Fletter of San Diego, California, who wrote a letter to us with the suggestion that we publish a prayer diary.

One Hour, a Bible, and an Open Mind

About the middle of my sophomore year at Agnes Scott College, I began keeping a journal, writing in it at the end of each day. I had already discovered that for me thoughts and inspirations flowed most readily at the point of a pencil. Ideas, convictions, emotions, yearnings were bubbling and seething, crying out for an outlet. The journal supplied that.

As the years went on, the first journal became a shelf full of them containing a potpourri of everything imaginable— the recordings of external events and concerns, fragments of poetry and quotations, vivid descriptions of people and places, Scripture promises, the record of my personal gropings for answers.

Meanwhile, toward the end of March 1943 came a watershed event in my life, therefore also for the journals. Declining health sent me to Johns Hopkins Hospital Clinic in Baltimore for a complete physical examination. After all the tests and X rays were completed, the day came to hear the specialist's report.

Moments before I was to walk into the doctor's office to get that verdict, God spoke to me. It was a gentle preparation for what lay ahead. I sensed that the news would not be good.

Passing years have blurred the exact words of the message, but the gist of it remains clear: *Body is irretrievably tied to spirit: physical health will always be dependent on spiritual health. For you, beginning every day with a quiet time with Me is essential.*

The message was given in such imperative terms that it obscured the fact that the Lord was also preparing me for the doctor's report. For the news was grim. I was to go home and go to bed—full-time.

During the next year and a half there was plenty of leisure for that morning "Quiet Hour." My gropings after truth were intensified by immense need. The journals ballooned apace.

In the years since then I have not always kept faith with this daily lifeline. But whenever I slip, I know what the trouble is and what to do about it.

When my husband, Peter Marshall, died so suddenly at 46, the journal notations recorded all the elements of heartache, fear, and discouragement experienced by any young widow with a nine-year-old son, together with the answers given me.

Then after ten years of widowhood, in 1959, Leonard LeSourd came into my life, drawing from me a new dimension of motherhood for his three young children. Inevitably the joining of two homes containing four children brought Len and me a multitude of new problems. Shortly after returning from our honeymoon, these adjustments threatened to overwhelm us.

How could we cope with the rebellion of a nineteen-year-old son away at Yale, the hostility of a ten-year-old daughter, and the discipline of two young boys, three and six, who had for years been subject to a series of housekeepers? Not to mention moving into a new house in a new community, seeking the right help, solving two career adjustments, and coping with myriad needs of family and relatives.

Aware that I was arising early each day, Len became curious. "Long ago I learned," I explained, "that I need time with the Lord every morning if I'm to keep my head above the water. For me, it's a must."

Len looked thoughtful. "That would be good for me too. We could set the alarm for thirty minutes earlier."

I shook my head. "That's not enough time."

He looked at me incredulously. But he too soon discovered that to fill our thoughts with the power and wisdom of Scripture, meditate on that, and pray adequately for our concerns, we needed a full hour before the children were up and the daily turmoil and confusion began.

Three simple purchases were made one winter day almost twenty years ago. I bought a small electric percolator, a timing device that would start it percolating whenever we set it, and a brown notebook for Len. These items were to shape our early morning hours for many years.

It was Len who began to keep a prayer log; we had so many prayer requests that we could not keep them all in our minds. Just as the "Quiet Hour" had been essential to me alone, now it became the stabilizing factor in our marriage. It has provided the setting in which we seek to grow in faith, to come closer to God and to build inner strength to withstand the fierce storms and satanic onslaughts that every person faces in life.

The basic tools are notebook, pen or pencil, and a Bible. Additional tools such as a concordance, Bible commentaries, and books on faith and prayer can all be helpful.

We conceived of this book as a way for an individual or a couple to get started on a devotional program that can lift and strengthen life. In a marriage, one can be the recorder, as Len was in our case, or both can keep separate spiritual diaries. I have continued to use my journal each day, filling it with my thoughts, plus what I feel the Lord is saying to me.

These are difficult, terrifying times. A simple faith, called upon only in emergencies, is not enough today. The attacks on morals, religious beliefs and standards of decency are shattering those who have no inner protection. Desperately we need the armor of God. But how can we put on the armor unless we are knowledgeable about the equipment provided us in the very real world of the spirit? Daily food in absorbing the Word of God is just as much needed as food for our bodies; daily communication face-to-face with the One who can help us and rescue us is indispensable.

An hour each day, a favorite translation of the Bible that you make your own by marking it, and the use of a resource diary like this one can start you on a prayer journey that will turn your problems into highways and make your life an adventure.

—Catherine Marshall

How This Book Can Help You Grow Spiritually

I began making lists as a college student at Ohio Wesleyan back in the late '30s: papers to write, personal items needed, girls to call for dates. Three years as a pilot in the Air Corps during World War II interrupted this process, but it began again when I became an editor at *Guideposts* magazine in 1946.

The years peeled off; *Guideposts* grew steadily through the late '40s and '50s. Each week began with a list of things to do: conferences with writers, articles to edit, staff meetings, family needs.

Early summer 1959 found me in a major crisis. A single parent with three children to rear, I went through eight housekeepers in two years. I simply could not handle my job and meet the needs of my young children alone. Something had to be done. Yet how could I know what God wanted for me? Or whether His plan could include a second marriage?

Alone in my bedroom late one night I closed my eyes and prayed. *Lord, what about it? I can't go on like this. Do You have anyone in mind for me?*

One name popped immediately into my thoughts—Catherine Marshall.

Surely, Lord, that isn't from You, I thought. I knew Catherine professionally but had placed her in a special category: highly spiritual. Her marriage to Peter Marshall had been movingly portrayed to millions in articles, a best-selling book, and a very successful motion picture.

However, in case the Lord really *was* guiding me, I made a date to see Catherine in Washington, D.C., letting her think that this meeting was for professional reasons. Though I found her warm and feminine, it was the facade of the professional woman that she presented to me.

I decided to try once more. This time for ten hours straight we talked on a summer day as we walked through Rock Creek Park west of Washington, picnicked alone, and drove along Skyline Drive. There was an incredible meshing together of beliefs, thoughts, and experiences. Four months later we were married.

As Catherine has already written, soon after our marriage we faced a staggering array of problems and difficulties. Catherine suggested teasingly that I needed a list to keep track of my lists. Our early morning prayer time together became the anchor point of each day.

What a joy to be awakened each day by the gentle sound and pleasant aroma of coffee percolating! By the time the coffee was ready, we were each surrounded by Bibles, books, my new brown notebook, and pencils. We each read quietly for the first half hour (sometimes in separate spots) then spent the second half hour on prayer work.

For it really was work. Most of the entries focused on Peter (nineteen), Linda (ten), Chester (six), and Jeff (three). The log that first day in our new home in Chappaqua, New York, contained these items:

Prayer Requests—December 15, 1959

1. That we locate the right housekeeper who can cook and who enjoys taking care of children.

13

2. That Catherine know how and when she is to continue writing *Christy*.
3. That Peter do more work and less playing around at Yale.
4. That Linda be less emotional about the clothes we ask her to wear and more interested in her studies.
5. That Chester stop fighting with his brother and accept his new home situation.
6. That we get Jeff toilet-trained.

Dozens of additional prayer requests filled the pages of the days that followed: a close relative with a drinking problem, a stealing problem at the office, a broken relationship with a neighbor, tensions with in-laws, guidance as to which church we should belong to, financial decisions involving family members. The items went on and on.

One day the request for the right housekeeper was answered. Through my mother we learned about Lucy, who made it possible for Catherine to resume her work on the novel *Christy*. In a separate page I wrote at the top: *Prayer Answers.* Underneath I made a notation about Lucy—and the date she began to work for us.

Soon we learned more about answers to prayer: specific requests yield precise answers. We didn't just ask for help with the house, we asked for live-in help, someone who would be warm, comfortable, a good cook, someone who liked children. We also discovered that unless we actually wrote down the *answers* to our prayers, we tended to accept them as occurring just in the natural course of events. With written notes marking prayer answers we found ourselves with deeper and more articulate gratitude. Not only that, watching those answers pile up, being able to look back in the log and see how ingeniously God had answered our prayer requests was a marvelous stimulus to faith.

The decision to arise early each morning for a time of prayer and Bible study was the turning point in our marriage, helping us resolve day-by-day tensions and upsets. Prayer forced us to face up to each situation. We could duck some problems for a while but not for long. The morning prayer period was also the time for an honest sharing of feelings between us. I discovered early that if I tried to present a controversial matter the night before, the adrenaline started flowing, the talk became charged, and Catherine would remain sleepless for hours after we turned out the light. Early morning in a prayer atmosphere was the time for confrontations.

What I learned from this prayer experience together began to shape my role as a husband. At the beginning of our marriage I had made two wrong assumptions. The first was that Catherine was better equipped to be the spiritual leader of our home since she knew more than I did about the Bible and was more articulate in prayer. But I soon learned, to my surprise, that these qualities do not qualify a wife for spiritual authority over her husband and children.

My second wrong assumption was that Catherine wanted this role. Not only did she resist it instinctively, but she did not want to go against the scriptural position that it is the husband's role to be "prophet" and "priest" for his own household.

Yet she also sensed that it would be a mistake to push me into a spiritual posture I did not want to assume. I belonged to the masculine school which held that because women were in the home more than men, they had better opportunities to provide children with religious teaching. When Catherine balked at the role I tried to assign her, the matter became one of our chief prayer concerns in our early morning time together.

It did not take me long to realize that unless I became the spiritual head of our home, Chester and Jeff would consider religion as something for the womenfolk. It was frightening to see how my sons copied everything I did: mannerisms, speech, attitudes toward work, food, church, sports. When I said grace and led the family prayer time, they were soon praying too, as if it were the natural thing to do. Despite my almost "bread and potatoes" prayers, I soon found myself quite comfortable in the role as spiritual head of our home.

And so our morning prayer period set the tone and direction for every day in our twenty-three years of marriage. We turned over our problems to the Lord. We committed ourselves to Him. We were submitted to each other. For two people with strong individualistic natures who could disagree on all manner of issues, the oneness that came during our early morning time together was the stabilizing factor in our marriage.

If you stay with your prayer time day by day, week by week, I believe the Lord will not only give you an adventuresome year, He will honor your faithfulness and bless your life.

—Leonard LeSourd

How to Use This Book

1. Set aside an hour each day, if possible, early in the morning. Then find a quiet place away from interruptions for prayer, reading, and meditation.
2. The basics are a Bible, pen or pencil, and a prayer log. Additional resources recommended: concordance, Bible commentary, one or more recent translations of the Bible to go with the King James edition.
3. Seek the depths of each day's Scripture. Ponder it. Ask the Lord to speak to you through it.
4. Use the prayer-meditations in this book as guidelines, improvising or adding to them as you see fit.
5. Seek to memorize one verse of Scripture each day. Three-by-five cards can be used to write down the verse. Carry each verse with you all day long and refer to it at free moments. In a matter of months you will have stored up a treasury of Bible wisdom that can be called upon in all kinds of situations.
6. For couples the following prayer procedure is suggested: (a) talk over the people and situations that you are concerned about until you decide how you want to pray; (b) then pray aloud together; (c) one or both should then write down the prayers.
7. When a prayer has been answered, record the answer. If you are not sure of the exact date, include it in the monthly summary page.

8. Prayer work is the main purpose of this book, but some may want to make daily notations of business and social events, including travel.
9. If you want to deal with a certain problem area in your life, check the listing of themes by date covered in the index and adjust the prayers and Bible verses to fit your schedule.
10. At the end of the year go back over each month, tally the results, and write a yearly prayer summary.

Quiet Times
with
Catherine Marshall

January

The Heart's Home

God's Word to Me

Prepare ye the way of the Lord, make straight in the desert a highway for our God.

Isaiah 40:3, KJV

But if we walk in the light as He is in the light, we have fellowship with one another, and the blood of Jesus Christ His Son cleanses us from all sin.

1 John 1:7, NKJV

Prayer-Meditation

Prepare my heart, Lord, to receive afresh the King of kings. Purge me with Your Holy Spirit that He may find a clean, warm, and responsive abode in me. Help me to face the new year with courage, enthusiasm, and faith.

Cleansing of the Heart

God's Word to Me

Create in me a clean heart, O God, and put a new and right spirit within me.

Psalm 51:10, RSV

I will give you a new heart and a new mind. I will take away your stubborn heart of stone and give you an obedient heart.

Ezekiel 36:26, TEV

Prayer-Meditation

Lord Jesus, we come to You now as little children. Dress us again in clean pinafores; make us tidy once more with the tidiness of true remorse and confession. O wash our hearts, that they may be clean again. Make us to know the strengthening joys of the Spirit and the newness of life that only You can give.

Peter Marshall

The Nature of God

God's Word to Me

He who has My command-
ments and keeps them, it is he
who loves Me.

John 14:21, NKJV

May the God of hope fill you
with all joy and peace in believing, so that you may abound in
hope by the power of the Holy
Spirit.

Romans 15:13, NRSV

Prayer-Meditation

Some unknown saint long
ago penned these words: "Perfect obedience would be perfect
happiness if only we had perfect
confidence in the power we
were obeying." Yet, Father, I
cannot trust You *like that* unless
I know You as You really are. As
this new year gets underway, I
ask now for that kind of unfold-
ing friendship with You.

The Nature of God

God's Word to Me

"Why do you ask me about what
is good?" Jesus replied. "There is
only One who is good."

Matthew 19:17, NIV

His divine power has given us
everything we need for life and
godliness through our knowledge of him who called us by his
own glory and goodness.

2 Peter 1:3, NIV

Read Psalm 107:1–9.

Prayer-Meditation

Father, I confess that I have
sometimes maligned You by
questioning why a loving God
would allow some of the awful
tragedies in our world. Or under
a cloak of piety and resignation
to Your will, I have attributed
black deeds to You that even simple good will would preclude.

I would now rest on Jesus'
own Word, His pledge to me,
that His Father and my Father is
good, incapable of anything but
goodness.

The Nature of God

God's Word to Me

Yes, from the time of the first existence of day and from this day forth I am He, and there is no one who can deliver out of My hand. I will work and who can hinder or reverse it?

Isaiah 43:13, AMP

Because you are my help, I sing in the shadow of your wings.

Psalm 63:7, NIV

Prayer-Meditation

As the marsh-hen secretly
    builds on the watery sod,
Behold I will build me a nest
    on the greatness of God.

Sidney Lanier

Father, Your greatness includes limitless power, perfect peace, unerring guidance, and all Your grace and strength to draw upon. Still I hesitate. Here I am living off the crumbs of Your bounty when I could have the whole loaf.

O Father, enlarge my vision. Give me faith.

The Nature of God

God's Word to Me

He who did not spare his own Son but gave him up for us all, will he not also give us all things with him?

Romans 8:32, RSV

O house of Jacob, come and let us walk in the light of the LORD.

Isaiah 2:5, NKJV

Prayer-Meditation

What glorious assurance that everything God asks me to do is for my own good and joy and best interests—not just "spiritual" good, but good as I understand it! It is an adventure to test this out for myself in daily life, to try obeying those inner nudges—though I may not at the time understand. Then I receive proof after proof of God's love and watch-care.

Lord, I would embark today on this adventure of practicing Your presence during every waking hour, trusting Your selfless love for me.

Obedience

God's Word to Me

So if you walk in My ways, to keep My statutes and My commandments . . . then I will lengthen your days.

1 Kings 3:14, NKJV

Let us hear the conclusion of the whole matter: Fear God and keep His commandments, for this is the whole duty of man.

Ecclesiastes 12:13, NKJV

Prayer-Meditation

I was meditating today, Lord, on how many I know who died early in life—sometimes violently—because they violated Your laws. Show me how to communicate this principle to my circle of family and friends, especially the young and the careless.

Hearing God's Voice

God's Word to Me

Be still, and know that I am God.

Psalm 46:10, NKJV

Now the LORD came and stood there, calling as before, "Samuel! Samuel!" And Samuel said, "Speak, for your servant is listening."

1 Samuel 3:10, NRSV

Prayer-Meditation

Where cross the crowded ways
    of life,
Where sound the cries of race
    and clan,
Above the noise of selfish
    strife,
We hear Thy voice, O Son of
    man!

Frank M. North

Lord, I remember today that prayer is a two-way street. After talking to You, I am to stop and listen and wait for Your marching orders.

The Word

God's Word to Me

By the word of the Lord the heavens were made, and all their host by the breath of his mouth.

Psalm 33:6, RSV

For the word of God is living and powerful, and sharper than any two-edged sword, piercing even to the division of soul and spirit, and of joints and marrow, and is a discerner of the thoughts and intents of the heart.

Hebrews 4:12, NKJV

Read John 1:1–3 and Colossians 1:15–17.

Prayer-Meditation

Lord, the creative power of Your spoken Word is awesome to me. And I begin to see that You have shared with all Your children this startling, creative (or destructive) power of words. This day enable me to use this sacred trust aright.

The Word

God's Word to Me

He has granted to us his precious and very great promises, that through these you may escape from the corruption that is in the world.

2 Peter 1:4, RSV

How great is your goodness, which you have stored up for those who fear you, which you bestow in the sight of men on those who take refuge in you.

Psalm 31:19, NIV

Prayer-Meditation

Lord, since You cannot lie (Titus 1:2) and since You are bound by Your own nature and by Your Word to keep Your promises (1 Kings 8:56), please help me to grasp the great truth that Scripture is a veritable treasure chest of promises to claim for my every need. I need Your guidance as to how I can use these days to accumulate my own cherished collection of these great promises.

Love

God's Word to Me

And [the Samaritan] went to him and bandaged his wounds, pouring on oil and wine; and he set him on his own animal, brought him to an inn, and took care of him.

Luke 10:34, NKJV

Do not neglect to show hospitality to strangers, for by this some have entertained angels without knowing it.

Hebrews 13:2, NASB

Prayer-Meditation

Help me to be like that Samaritan, Lord, who did not seek counsel or approval from others before he reached out to help the injured man. Nor did he consider anything but the welfare of the one he helped. Instead he offered the same compassion You offered to the blind, the sick, the maimed and sin-weary people as You walked the roads of earth.

Open My Ears

God's Word to Me

Now when the chief priests and Pharisees heard His parables, they perceived that He was speaking of them.

Matthew 21:45, NKJV

Then the disciples came and said to Him, Do You know that the Pharisees were displeased and offended and indignant when they heard this saying?

Matthew 15:12, AMP

Prayer-Meditation

Jesus, I am convicted by the fact that even the priests and the Pharisees were more perceptive than I have often been. I usually think of someone else whom Your teaching fits, not me. I see now that Your Word applies especially to me. Help me to absorb and act upon it.

Joy

God's Word to Me

. . . Weeping may endure for a night, but joy comes in the morning.

Psalm 30:5, NKJV

But You, O LORD, are a shield for me, my glory and the One who lifts up my head.

Psalm 3:3, NKJV

Prayer-Meditation

Lord, I can stand almost anything when I know it to be temporary. Even in the midst of my weeping, when I look into Your eyes, I always experience the lift to my spirit of Your light touch. And I seem to hear You say, "Why are you so troubled? There's nothing here I can't handle!"

O Lord Jesus, thank You for the gift of Your clear-eyed perspective. It is priceless to me.

Tithing

God's Word to Me

Bring the full tithes into the storehouse, that there may be food in my house; and thereby put me to the test, says the LORD of hosts, if I will not open the windows of heaven for you and pour down for you an overflowing blessing.

Malachi 3:10, RSV

The LORD will establish you as his holy people, as he promised you on oath, if you keep the commands of the LORD your God and walk in his ways.

Deuteronomy 28:9, NIV

Prayer-Meditation

What an exciting challenge, Lord! People in every century have proved in their own experience that we can never outgive You. Yet I grieve for those who so shortchange themselves by holding so tightly to what they possess. How can anyone refuse Your blessing, Lord, by closing his windows to heaven?

Priority in Prayer

God's Word to Me

And when He had sent them away, He departed to the mountain to pray.

Mark 6:46, NKJV

One day Jesus was praying in a certain place. When he finished, one of his disciples said to him, "Lord, teach us to pray, just as John taught his disciples."

Luke 11:1, NIV

Prayer-Meditation

Jesus' earthly life as recorded in the Gospels has so much to teach me in the matter of priorities. For Him, prayer with His Father had top priority. This alone would pull Him away from those still unhealed or in need (Luke 4:42–43). Jesus used prayer: for regular communion with God (Mark 1:35); to seek God's will (Luke 22:41–42); for refreshment of body and spirit (Mark 6:46–47).

Lord, teach me about the perfect balance You demonstrated between "busyness" and quietness, between service and prayer.

Positive Prayer

God's Word to Me

You do not have, because you do not ask.

James 4:2, RSV

Read Matthew 6:7–8.

Prayer-Meditation

Jesus assured us that our Father knows what we need before we ask Him (Matthew 6:8). Why then should I pray? Because in giving me free will, God made the fulfilling of His plans for me dependent upon my cooperation. Then He gave me the privilege of being a creator in partnership with the Creator Himself. This means that the whole thrust of God's nature is always positive—never negative.

Father, I am ashamed that so many of my prayer requests are negative—to get rid of something. Help me from now on to get on with the thrust of creativity, moving always upward.

Blocks to Prayer

God's Word to Me

Likewise you husbands, dwell with them with understanding, giving honor to the wife, as to the weaker vessel, and as being heirs together of the grace of life, that your prayers may not be hindered.

1 Peter 3:7, NKJV

Therefore a man leaves his father and his mother and clings to his wife, and they become one flesh.

Genesis 2:24, NRSV

Prayer-Meditation

Lord, are You saying that an unharmonious relationship between husband and wife is a block to prayer? *Being heirs together of the grace of life* is such a beautiful picture of Your ideal of marriage that I will hold it before me in all my prayers for troubled marital relationships.

Prayer in Secret

God's Word to Me

When you pray, go into your room, and when you have shut your door, pray to your Father who is in the secret place; and your Father who sees in secret will reward you openly.

Matthew 6:6, NKJV

Read Isaiah 45:3; Mark 7:36; Matthew 9:30.

Prayer-Meditation

Lord, here You are instructing me in a principle, one of God's immutable laws of the universe: there is additional spiritual power in secrecy. Or conversely, creative power is dissipated by talking about it too soon.

This gives yet another exciting dimension to prayer. What adventure to enter into a secret prayer conspiracy with You and then see the joyous results exhibited for all to see!

Prayer without Ceasing

God's Word to Me

Pray continually; give thanks in all circumstances, for this is God's will for you in Christ Jesus.

1 Thessalonians 5:17–18, NIV

I want men everywhere to lift up holy hands in prayer, without anger or disputing.

1 Timothy 2:8, NIV

Prayer-Meditation

Instead of saying, as I often do, "I really should pray about so-and-so" (meaning some-time) or "I must remember to pray for Tom's diabetes," the scriptural injunction is *to pray now*. To pray "in every place" means while I'm driving the car, talking on the telephone, walking on the beach—wherever I am.

Depression

God's Word to Me

Rise, let us be going.

Matthew 26:46, NKJV

So he said, "I have been very zealous for the LORD God of hosts; for the children of Israel have forsaken Your covenant, torn down Your altars, and killed Your prophets with the sword. I alone am left; and they seek to take my life."

1 Kings 19:10, NKJV

Prayer-Meditation

Being depressed sometimes is simply part of our human-ness. Otherwise, we would have no capacity for joy, inspiration, and exaltation. Thus the Bible is peppered with accounts of the depressed: Elijah, Job, King David, Jonah, Joshua, Jesus' apostles.

Thank You, Father, for giving me a prescription for my depres-sion: I am to stop analyzing myself, rise, and perform the next commonplace task at hand "as unto the Lord." Thank You that as I take this initiative, You will return perspective and joy to me.

Jesus, the Answer

God's Word to Me

. . . until Christ be formed in you!

Galatians 4:19, RSV

But the fruit of the Spirit is love, joy, peace, patience, kindness, goodness, faithfulness, gentleness and self-control.

Galatians 5:22–23a, NIV

Prayer-Meditation

O Lord Jesus, I do not need patience or self-control, or even love today; what I really need is You . . . Your life lived out through mine until Your very likeness is reproduced in my life. And then You will be everything that I need: patience . . . self-control . . . love, and all the other fruits. You, Lord Jesus, are the One answer to my every need.

Patience

God's Word to Me

Because you have kept My command to persevere, I also will keep you from the hour of trial.

Revelation 3:10, NKJV

The LORD your God you shall follow, him alone you shall fear, his commandments you shall keep, his voice you shall obey, him you shall serve, and to him you shall hold fast.

Deuteronomy 13:4, NRSV

Prayer-Meditation

God is saying in this revelation that we are to hold fast to our faith in Him. Though our prayers have not been answered, though we have been tested to our limits, we are to be patient. We are to trust Him. In turn, He will honor our steadfastness, but always in His timing, not ours.

Lord, I pray for the inner strength to keep my relationship with You intact, regardless of what it costs me.

Pleasing Jesus

God's Word to Me

She has done a beautiful thing to me.

Mark 14:6, RSV

Then Mary took a pound of very costly oil of spikenard, anointed the feet of Jesus, and wiped his feet with her hair. And the house was filled with the fragrance of the oil.

John 12:3, NKJV

Prayer-Meditation

O Lord, grant me the satisfaction of pleasing You; not in work *for* You primarily, but in relationship *with* You. I would be like the woman who spent herself totally, wastefully, on Your behalf. Cause my single-minded goal to be that of satisfying You first. Then will my longing heart be filled with a love relationship with You.

Freedom in Jesus

God's Word to Me

If you continue in my word, you are truly my disciples, and you will know the truth, and the truth will make you free. . . . So if the Son makes you free, you will be free indeed.

John 8:31–32, 36, RSV

Now the Lord is the Spirit, and where the Spirit of the Lord is, there is liberty—emancipation from bondage, freedom.

2 Corinthians 3:17, AMP

Prayer-Meditation

Lord Jesus, You of all men were the most free because You were totally free of self-love.

Free me, Lord, from the darkness of lonely isolation. Free me from everything that holds me in crippling fear and worry so that I can give myself in child-like abandonment to You. Free me, Lord, to make choices so that You, not I, are at the center of my life.

Temptation

God's Word to Me

And now he [Jesus] can help those who are tempted, because he himself was tempted and suffered.

Hebrews 2:18, TEV

When tempted, no one should say, "God is tempting me." For God cannot be tempted by evil, nor does he tempt anyone.

James 1:13, NIV

Prayer-Meditation

To be tempted, I know, is not synonymous with sinning; rather, temptation is the inheritance of the human race. Further, I am tempted only by those things of which I am capable and even susceptible.

Lord, help me to see in each temptation the mark of Your trust in me to grow above it—not to be ensnared by it.

Temptation

God's Word to Me

Blessed is the man who endures temptation; for when he has been proved, he will receive the crown of life.

James 1:12, NKJV

If we have died with him, we will also live with him; if we endure, we will also reign with him.

2 Timothy 2:11b–12a, NRSV

Prayer-Meditation

Temptation is not something we can escape. The key word here is to *endure*. The craving comes, our nature wants to give in to it, but we know we should not. So we endure (resist) the desire until it leaves. Victory!

Temptation overcome has a sweetness to it, and heaven's reward is the crown of life.

Temptation

God's Word to Me

Each person is tempted when he is lured and enticed by his own desire.

James 1:14, RSV

Read Matthew 4:1–11; Ephesians 6:12.

Prayer-Meditation

Satan's goal is to defeat us any way he can. He aims to fit both the taste and the capability of each one of us: what is not attractive to *us* would obviously be no temptation at all; neither would ambitions so far beyond us as to be ludicrous. Note how even with Jesus this same pattern was followed: to the Lord of glory Satan offered nothing less than "all the kingdoms of the world."

Lord, give me an awareness that Satan knows *me*—my tastes and particular ambitions—and along with that awareness give me Your strength in resisting him.

Love One Another

God's Word to Me

Be kindly affectionate to one another with brotherly love, in honor giving preference to one another.

Romans 12:10, NKJV

"This is what the LORD Almighty says: 'Administer true justice; show mercy and compassion to one another.'"

Zechariah 7:9, NIV

Prayer-Meditation

Lord, I'm glad You said that. There have been times when I have so longed for a Christian brother or sister who would love me enough to be interested in sharing his or her dreams and difficulties, joys and sorrows with me. Help me to be sensitive, Father, to that one person who right now needs my love and understanding.

His Presence Satisfies

God's Word to Me

Draw near to God and He will draw near to you.

James 4:8, NKJV

Let us draw near to God with a sincere heart in full assurance of faith, having our hearts sprinkled to cleanse us from a guilty conscience and having our bodies washed with pure water.

Hebrews 10:22, NIV

Prayer-Meditation

The Word is so simple, Lord. Why do I always try to make it complex? When I am feeling lost, alone, bereft, cannot feel Your presence—even when I am most reluctant to pray—that is precisely when I need most to draw near to You. I praise You for Your sure promise that when I do, You *will* respond, You *will* draw near to me.

Dreams and Visions

God's Word to Me

And it shall come to pass afterward that I will pour out My Spirit on all flesh. . . . Your old men shall dream dreams, your young men shall see visions.

Joel 2:28, NKJV

But those who wait on the LORD shall renew their strength; they shall mount up with wings like eagles, they shall run and not be weary, they shall walk and not faint.

Isaiah 40:31, NKJV

Read Acts 2:1–21.

Prayer-Meditation

How marvelously You will bridge the span of life for me, Lord. In my youth You will paint brilliant pictures of opportunities full of stimulating challenge, needing the vigor of youth to achieve. Then when the strength of my flesh has diminished, gently You will encourage me with dreams that continually refuel the bright light of hope.

The New Life

God's Word to Me

I can do all things in him who strengthens me.

> Philippians 4:13, RSV

But he said to me, "My grace is sufficient for you, for my power is made perfect in weakness." So, I will boast all the more gladly of my weaknesses, so that the power of Christ may dwell in me.

> 2 Corinthians 12:9, NRSV

Read Romans 8:2.

Prayer-Meditation

Christ has changed all our "cannots" into "can do's."

O Lord, I have tasted a bit of the power of Your new life to overcome old ways. Through yielding to Your Spirit, You have enabled me to do things I never thought possible. For where I was bound before, now in You I am free. My strength may be insufficient for the tasks You will call me to today, but the power that upholds the universe can handle all my needs. Keep me in the stream of Your strengthening, enabling life.

My Prayer Requests

God's Answers

February

Spiritual Vision

God's Word to Me

[Moses said to the Lord] If I have found favor in your eyes, teach me your ways so I may know you and continue to find favor with you.

Exodus 33:13, NIV

Moses answered the people, "Do not be afraid. Stand firm and you will see the deliverance the LORD will bring you today. The Egyptians you see today you will never see again."

Exodus 14:13, NIV

Prayer-Meditation

As the Lord comforted and emboldened Moses, I too need reassurance and direction.

Lord, enlarge my spiritual vision that I may see Your presence and Your glory in all areas of my life.

Nature of God

God's Word to Me

Then God saw everything that He had made, and indeed it was very good.... For every creature of God is good, and nothing is to be refused if it is received with thanksgiving; for it is sanctified by the word of God and prayer.

Genesis 1:31;
1 Timothy 4:4–5, NKJV

He has made everything beautiful in its time. He has also set eternity in the hearts of men; yet they cannot fathom what God has done from beginning to end.

Ecclesiastes 3:11, NIV

Prayer-Meditation

Lord, please give me new eyes to see the good in all Your creation . . . the rich color of a single rose, the faithfulness in the eyes of a pet, the potential for good in every person I know. Activate, O Lord, the sensitivity in me to see something of You in every person I meet.

Winter of the Spirit

God's Word to Me

Now it was the Feast of Dedication in Jerusalem, and it was winter.

John 10:22, NKJV

For the winter is past, the rain is over and gone. The flowers are springing up and the time of the singing of birds has come.

Song of Solomon 2:11–12, TLB

Prayer-Meditation

Winter speaks of deadness of spirit. The spiritually dead were the ones who crucified the Son of God.

If there is any deadness in my spirit, Lord, come with Your resurrection power that I may be restored to what I was in You from the beginning.

For the Troubled

God's Word to Me

Then I will restore her . . . and make the dale of Trouble a door of hope.

Hosea 2:15, MOFFATT

I know that You can do everything, and that no purpose of Yours can be withheld from You.

Job 42:2, NKJV

Read Genesis 45:1–8.

Prayer-Meditation

It helps so much to know that before any upsetting event reaches us, God already has a plan by which He can bring good out of the difficulty (Romans 8:28). God wants to use trouble as the starting point for new creativity.

Father, how sorely I need this assurance, knowing that You are the only One who can make my dale of trouble a door of hope. I praise You that in the end, no evil can defeat the Lord of my life.

41

Faith

God's Word to Me

But without faith it is impossible to please Him, for he who comes to God must believe that He is . . . a rewarder of those who diligently seek Him.

Hebrews 11:6, NKJV

Immediately the father of the child cried out, "I believe; help my unbelief!"

Mark 9:24, NRSV

Prayer-Meditation

The apostles' cry to You, Lord Jesus, was "Give us more faith." They saw this as the most urgent need of their lives because of Your own attitude about it: healing depends on faith (Matthew 9:29; Luke 8:50); the forgiveness of sins comes through faith (Luke 5:20; 7:50). As You controlled the elements, You asked the disciples, "Where is your faith?" (Luke 8:25).

Lord, in the days and weeks ahead, I too want to strengthen my faith. I open myself for Your teaching, Lord. I commit myself to a time of prayer each day for this purpose.

Faith

God's Word to Me

Looking unto Jesus, the author and finisher of our faith. . . .

Hebrews 12:2, NKJV

To one there is given through the Spirit the message of wisdom, to another the message of knowledge by means of the same Spirit, to another faith by the same Spirit. . . .

1 Corinthians 12:8–9a, NIV

Prayer-Meditation

Lord, I know that I can no more get on in my Christian life without faith than a fish can survive out of water.

Since the apostle Paul tells us that faith can only come as a gift of the Holy Spirit, it occurs to me that I have never specifically asked for the gift of faith.

I ask now, Lord Jesus, and thank You in advance for this great gift.

Faith

God's Word to Me

So then faith comes by hearing, and hearing by the word of God.

Romans 10:17, NKJV

Stand in the gate of the LORD's house, and proclaim there this word, and say, Hear the word of the LORD, all you people of Judah, you that enter these gates to worship the LORD.

Jeremiah 7:2, NRSV

Prayer-Meditation

This morning Your Word is telling me, Lord, that my faith can be nourished through two strong channels: Scripture and hearing Your Word proclaimed by those preachers who have been truly "sent" by You.

I see that I need Scripture because (1) I cannot claim God's promises for myself until I know what He has promised, and (2) the Bible is the story of God's dealings with people like me.

Lead me, Lord, to those proclaimers of the Word who are the "sent" ones.

Faith

God's Word to Me

Far better to rely on the Eternal than put faith in men.

Psalm 118:8, MOFFATT

For whatever is born of God overcomes the world. And this is the victory that has overcome the world—our faith.

1 John 5:4, NKJV

Prayer-Meditation

My tendency, Lord, is not to rely on God alone until circumstances force me to do so. How often I have said, "Of course I believe that God can do anything, but. . . ." The "but" reveals that my faith has not gone beyond intellectual belief.

Show me one area today, Lord, where You want me to rely on You alone without trying to work out my own salvation.

Spiritual Warfare

God's Word to Me

He [Jesus] knew what was in man.

John 2:25, NKJV

Prayer-Meditation

It is no doubt impossible to prevent his praying for his mother, but we [the forces of Satan] have means of rendering the prayers innocuous. Make sure that they are always very "spiritual," that he is always concerned with the state of her soul and never with her rheumatism.

C. S. Lewis
from *The Screwtape Letters*

Lord Jesus, You know only too well our inclination at times to be super-spiritual and pompous—and how this makes us easy prey for Satan. Teach us to resist the enemy through the truth of Your Word and incisive, persistent prayer.

Cry of the Human Heart

God's Word to Me

My God, My God, why have You forsaken Me?

Psalm 22:1, NKJV

Restore to me the joy of your salvation and grant me a willing spirit, to sustain me.

Psalm 51:12, NIV

Prayer-Meditation

King David's lament is the cry of the sinner who has lost contact with his Lord and wants to be restored. Have we not all been there?

The good news is that the Lord does hear this cry. He listens to the heart and if there is honest repentance, He lifts the barrier, forgives the sin, and, as He did with David, restores the relationship.

Thank You, Lord, for hearing our hearts' cry.

The Listening Heart

God's Word to Me

Speak, Lord, for Your servant hears.

1 Samuel 3:9, NKJV

Your hands have made and fashioned me; give me understanding that I may learn your commandments.

Psalm 119:73, NRSV

Prayer-Meditation

Lord, when I have spilled out to You my concerns and needs, my prayer has only just begun. What You have to say to me is of far more importance. So I wait now with mind and heart open to Your voice, ready to heed and to obey.

Love

God's Word to Me

Greater love has no one than this, than to lay down one's life for his friends.

John 15:13, NKJV

This is how we know what love is: Jesus Christ laid down his life for us. And we ought to lay down our lives for our brothers.

1 John 3:16, NIV

Prayer-Meditation

Lord, my life consists of my desires, my needs, my demands, my opinions. You are asking me to lay these aside on behalf of my family and friends. It's easier to do, Jesus, when Your love is in my heart. Give me Your kind of life-giving love.

And when I am tempted to self-pity in my giving and serving, grant that I may hear Your words: "This is the greatest form of love and it pleases Me."

Patience

God's Word to Me

Knowing that the testing of your faith produces patience . . . let patience have its perfect work.

James 1:3–4, NKJV

He who is slow to wrath has great understanding, but he who is impulsive exalts folly.

Proverbs 14:29, NKJV

Prayer-Meditation

Deliver us, O Lord, from the foolishness of impatience. Let us not be in such a hurry as to run on without Thee. Slow us down, O Lord, that we may take time to think, time to pray, and time to find out Thy will.

Peter Marshall

Praying Parents

God's Word to Me

For the promise [of the gift of the Holy Spirit] is to you and to your children . . . as many as the Lord our God will call.

Acts 2:39, NKJV

We will tell to the coming generation the glorious deeds of the LORD, and his might, and the wonders that he has done.

Psalm 78:4b, NRSV

Prayer-Meditation

Praise You, Lord, for this promise. So many parents who have come to know You as Savior are trying to make up through prayer for all the wasted years when they could have been teaching their children at Your feet. Thank You that as the good Shepherd You will find all these lost sheep and bring them to the Kingdom.

Obedient Children

God's Word to Me

Children, obey your parents . . . for this is well-pleasing to the Lord.

Colossians 3:20, AMP

Honor your father and your mother, so that you may live long in the land the LORD your God is giving you.

Exodus 20:12, NIV

Read Matthew 15:3–6.

Prayer-Meditation

The promise here is that children who honor and obey their parents will have a long and blessed life (Exodus 20:12). How do we pray for rebellious children? My heart goes out to all young people who do not know You, Father, because they never got along with their earthly fathers.

Living in the Present

God's Word to Me

Therefore do not be anxious about tomorrow. . . . Let the day's own trouble be sufficient for the day.

Matthew 6:34, RSV

Instead, you ought to say, "If it is the Lord's will, we will live and do this or that."

James 4:15, NIV

Prayer-Meditation

Let us perform our concerns and duties with laughter and kind faces, let cheerfulness abound with industry. Give us to go blithely on our business all this day. . . . Give us courage and gaiety and the quiet mind.

Robert Louis Stevenson

Lord, enable me and my family to savor today the joy of living fully in the present moment.

Mercy

God's Word to Me

Blessed are the merciful, for they shall obtain mercy.

Matthew 5:7, NKJV

And he said, "I will make all my goodness pass before you, and will proclaim before you the name, 'The LORD'; and I will be gracious to whom I will be gracious, and will show mercy on whom I will show mercy."

Exodus 33:19, NRSV

Prayer-Meditation

Since God has long been in the business of showing mercy to His creatures, He gives a special blessing to those who demonstrate it to others. Grace flows from mercy as its fountain.

Thank You, Lord, that Your mercy is everlasting, that it may even come to us when we don't deserve it.

Witnessing

God's Word to Me

Now therefore, go, and I will be with your mouth and teach you what you shall say.

Exodus 4:12, NKJV

For I could wish that I myself were accursed and cut off and banished from Christ, for the sake of my brethren and instead of them, my natural kinsmen and my fellow countrymen.

Romans 9:3, AMP

Prayer-Meditation

Lord, I am concerned about members of my family and friends whose lives are adrift because they do not know You. I am eager to present You to others. But my eagerness could be a hindrance and an offense unless fully controlled by Your Holy Spirit. So I ask that as You promised Moses to be with his mouth, so You will also be with me to give me the words to bring sinners to repentance and to build up believers.

God's Love

God's Word to Me

Love does not insist on its own way.

1 Corinthians 13:5, RSV

And so we know and rely on the love God has for us. God is love. Whoever lives in love lives in God, and God in him.

1 John 4:16, NIV

Read John 17:24.

Prayer-Meditation

On the human level, one of love's most obvious characteristics is unselfishness. Since God is all love—is of the essence of love—can His love be of a different caliber? The truth is that God is not only unselfish, He is selfless. His every thought, purpose, and plan since the beginning of time has been for His children's welfare and happiness.

Father, I am ashamed that at times I have actually been afraid of You. Give me now faith in Your selfless love for me.

Praising God

God's Word to Me

Then God saw everything that He had made, and indeed it was very good.

Genesis 1:31, NKJV

O LORD, how many are Thy works! In wisdom Thou hast made them all; the earth is full of Thy possessions.

Psalm 104:24, NASB

Prayer-Meditation

Creator Spirit . . . forbid that I should walk through Thy beautiful world with unseeing eyes:

Forbid that the lure of the market-place should ever entirely steal my heart away from the love of the open acres and the green trees. . . .

Forbid that when all Thy creatures are greeting the morning with songs and shouts of joy, I alone should wear a dull and sullen face. . . .

I praise Thee, Creator-God.

John Baillie

The Word

God's Word to Me

So shall My word be that goes forth from My mouth; it shall not return to Me void, but it shall accomplish what I please.

Isaiah 55:11, NKJV

Long ago God spoke to our ancestors in many and various ways by the prophets, but in these last days he has spoken to us by a Son, whom he appointed heir of all things, through whom he also created the worlds.

Hebrews 1:1–2, NRSV

Read John 10:35.

Prayer-Meditation

Gratefully, I accept Your Word as bedrock truth—a final anchor point in this confused and troubled world. Beginning this day, Lord, teach me how to distinguish Your Word from all the other words that come at me from so many different sources.

Faith

God's Word to Me

Woe to those who go down to Egypt for help and rely on horses, and trust in chariots because they are many and in horsemen because they are very strong, but they look not to the Holy One of Israel nor seek and consult the Lord!

Isaiah 31:1, AMP

Read Isaiah 12:2.

Prayer-Meditation

Our constant temptation is to trust in the "chariots of Egypt" or in other words, in earthly resources!

We can *see* them; they are real and look substantial, while God's chariots are invisible and . . . it is hard to believe they are there.

Hannah Whitall Smith

Father, You know my longtime concern about the salvation of _____. Open my eyes to see Your chariots rather than pinning my faith on earthly resources.

God's Guidance

God's Word to Me

Commit your way to the Lord, trust also in Him, and He shall bring it to pass.

Psalm 37:5, NKJV

In all your ways acknowledge Him, and He shall direct your paths.

Proverbs 3:6, NKJV

Prayer-Meditation

Take, O Lord, and receive my entire liberty, my memory, my understanding, and my whole will.

All that I am, all that I have, Thou hast given me, and I will give it back again to Thee to be disposed of according to Thy good pleasure. Give me only Thy love and Thy grace; with Thee I am rich enough, nor do I ask for ought besides.

St. Ignatius Loyola

Freedom and Authority

God's Word to Me

But Peter and the apostles answered, "We must obey God rather than men."

Acts 5:29, RSV

But even if we or an angel from heaven should preach a gospel other than the one we preached to you, let him be eternally condemned!

Galatians 1:8, NIV

Prayer-Meditation

Father, thank You for leading me to this verse as it applies to the many communities and cults springing up today. Does any leader seek to usurp or subtract from the final supremacy of Jesus' Lordship for me? Would rules of or vows to this group stand between me and the direct guidance of the Holy Spirit?

Thank You, Father, that you want only sturdy disciples growing steadily in Your strength and Your freedom, dependent upon no person.

His Forgiveness

God's Word to Me

A woman who had lived a sinful life . . . began to wet his feet with her tears. Then she wiped them with her hair.

Luke 7:37–38, NIV

So overflowing is his kindness toward us that he took away all our sins through the blood of his Son, by whom we are saved.

Ephesians 1:7, TLB

Prayer-Meditation

What a picture of depression! This woman had no self-esteem; she had no concern about becoming a public spectacle. But neither did she luxuriate in self-pity. She came to Jesus, poured out all her longings—her repentance for sin confessed by her actions—and found forgiveness and absolution beyond her wildest dreams.

"Your faith has saved you; go in peace."

Thank You, Lord.

Keeping Power

God's Word to Me

Those whom You gave Me I have kept; and none of them is lost. . . .

John 17:12, NKJV

I give them eternal life, and they will never perish. No one will snatch them out of my hand.

John 10:28, NRSV

Prayer-Meditation

How reassuring it is, Father, to recognize that in spite of my failure to live up to Your Word, in spite of my surrendering to temptation on occasion, in spite of all the errancy of my humanity, I am still secure in You because of my relationship in Jesus.

Thank You for including in Scripture such people as Peter, Thomas, Mary Magdalene, James, John, David, and many others who sinned but in repentance turned again to You and were restored to full fellowship with You. Thank You that I too may come this way.

Prayer for New Believers

God's Word to Me

You once walked according to the course of this world . . . sons of disobedience. . . .

Ephesians 2:2, NKJV

Read John 17:15.

Prayer-Meditation

This morning, Father, I would pray for _____, who is a new person in Christ Jesus. He/she is so new to Your kingdom and is not finding it easy to leave behind old habits, former companions, the stimuli and enticements of a world so at cross-purposes with Your purposes. Lord, strengthen _____ and other new struggling Christians as well. Help them quickly to recognize and relinquish to You all the enticements of the old life: certain types of music, reading, and television; certain atmospheres, people—whatever. Be their "Remembrancer" who can alert them to the dangers and lead them to a safe place.

Trust

God's Word to Me

Brethren, I do not count myself to have apprehended; but one thing I do, forgetting those things which are behind and reaching forward to those things which are ahead, I press toward the goal.

Philippians 3:13–14, NKJV

Then Jesus said to Simon, "Don't be afraid; from now on you will catch men." So they pulled their boats up on shore, left everything and followed him.

Luke 5:10b–11, NIV

Prayer-Meditation

Father, when understanding eludes me as I struggle to find meaning in some of the circumstances of life, I am encouraged by Paul's statement here. Give me that adventurous faith that will move on ahead, trusting You to lead and ultimately to give understanding.

My Prayer Requests

_____

_____

_____

_____

_____

_____

_____

_____

_____

God's Answers

_____

_____

_____

_____

_____

_____

_____

_____

_____

_____

March

Christ's Humanity

God's Word to Me

And the Word became flesh and dwelt among us.

John 1:14, NKJV

And being found in human form, he humbled himself and became obedient to the point of death—even death on a cross.

Philippians 2:7b–8, NRSV

Prayer-Meditation

Lord Jesus, how I praise You for being willing to take the form of a servant, to be the Son of man in true humanity. How grateful I am that You have walked every dusty, weary, lonesome, frightening trail of earthly life ahead of me. Otherwise, Lord, You could be for me only a figure in a stained-glass window or a spotless statue in a niche—inaccessible, unapproachable.

Protection

God's Word to Me

Put on the whole armor of God . . . having shod your feet with the equipment of the gospel of peace.

Ephesians 6:11, 15, RSV

I will give you the keys of the kingdom of heaven; whatever you bind on earth will be bound in heaven, and whatever you loose on earth will be loosed in heaven.

Matthew 16:19, NIV

Prayer-Meditation

I pondered this for some time, Lord, until I saw that to protect ourselves from attack we must first be aggressive evangelists. Equip me with the love and boldness I need as I remember that the objective of our warfare is the destruction of evil and the coming of the kingdom of peace (the kingdom of right relationships) into every area of my life.

Loneliness

God's Word to Me

A little that a righteous man has is better than the riches of many wicked.

Psalm 37:16, NKJV

You, O LORD, are the portion of my inheritance and my cup; You maintain my lot.

Psalm 16:5, NKJV

Prayer-Meditation

I watched her enter the room. Perhaps about fifty, I thought. Attractively groomed, color-streaked hair framed her suntanned face. Her expensive clothing and her trim figure belied her years. But it was her utter loneliness that caught at my heart. From her nervous chatter I glimpsed in the background a husband, a child; yet her life seemed strangely empty, devoid of purpose.

O Jesus, I pray that she will meet You.

Sharing the Good News

God's Word to Me

I am ready to preach the gospel. . . . For I am not ashamed of the gospel of Christ, for it is the power of God to salvation for everyone who believes.

Romans 1:15–16, NKJV

But God chose the foolish things of the world to shame the wise; God chose the weak things of the world to shame the strong.

1 Corinthians 1:27, NIV

Prayer-Meditation

I confess, Lord, that there have been times when I was embarrassed, yes, even a bit ashamed to speak Your name. Forgive me for this cowardice; empower me with the courage to testify and the wisdom to know the right moment.

Christian Growth

God's Word to Me

Love your enemies.

Matthew 5:44, RSV

Do not lay up for yourselves treasures on earth. . . . Do not be anxious about tomorrow.

Matthew 6:19, 34, RSV

Prayer-Meditation

Lord Jesus, what an impossible ethic You have given us in the Sermon on the Mount! Even as these words of teaching first fell from Your lips, You knew that the bravest human effort, the greatest willpower would never come close to achieving this. Even then the Cross loomed ahead and, beyond that, a glorious resurrection, and, finally, the sending of the Holy Spirit.

Now I understand: from the beginning You knew that this impossible ethic made no sense apart from the enabling power of Your Spirit inside me to live it out. For instance, when I cannot possibly love my enemy, You, inside me, can—and will. Praise You, Jesus, for that!

The Tongue

God's Word to Me

Let your speech always be gracious, seasoned with salt, so that you may know how you ought to answer every one.

Colossians 4:6, RSV

And we sent Timothy, our brother and co-worker for God in proclaiming the gospel of Christ, to strengthen and encourage you for the sake of your faith, so that no one would be shaken by these persecutions.

1 Thessalonians 3:2–3a, NRSV

Prayer-Meditation

Lord, I've prayed for Your Spirit to enter my heart. Now I ask for You to sweeten the timbre of my voice to reflect perfectly Your love as You use my mouth to comfort the afflicted, to encourage the downhearted, to inspire the defeated.

Let my words to others be only for their upbuilding and encouragement and consolation, savoring of Your never-failing, loving graciousness to me.

Prayer for Small Needs

God's Word to Me

Your Father knows what you need before you ask him.

Matthew 6:8, RSV

What man among you, if he has a hundred sheep and has lost one of them, does not leave the ninety-nine in the open pasture, and go after the one which is lost, until he finds it?

Luke 15:4, NASB

Prayer-Meditation

Sometimes I have thought it selfish to pray about the petty details of everyday living. But the total stream of our lives is the sum of just such minutiae. And Jesus concerned Himself with those very things: people's health problems, securing the money for Peter's tax, a woman who had lost one coin, one little lost sheep, the contents of a little boy's lunch box so that a hungry crowd could be fed.

Father, this tremendous truth that You care about my life like that seems too good to be true. I praise You that it is too good *not* to be true.

Intercession

God's Word to Me

But I have prayed for you, that your faith should not fail.

Luke 22:32, NKJV

In him we were also chosen, having been predestined according to the plan of him who works out everything in conformity with the purpose of his will, in order that we, who were the first to hope in Christ, might be for the praise of his glory.

Ephesians 1:11–12, NIV

Read Luke 22:54–62.

Prayer-Meditation

Lord, this morning, greatly concerned about _____, I would pray for my friend. Suddenly, I see that the key to answered prayer for another is *my* faith that You do have a beautiful, joyous plan for each one of us, and that Your power can foil all of Satan's attempts to interfere with that plan. As I pray for _____, how wonderful that You lift my eyes from any evaluation of mine about _____, to focus on *Your* strength and power.

Constant Prayer

God's Word to Me

I desire then that in every place the men should pray.... Rejoice always, pray constantly.

1 Timothy 2:8;
1 Thessalonians 5:16–17, RSV

Pray at all times—on every occasion, in every season—in the Spirit, with all [manner of] prayer and entreaty. To that end keep alert and watch with strong purpose and perseverance, interceding in behalf of all the saints (God's consecrated people).

Ephesians 6:18, AMP

Prayer-Meditation

In order to pray constantly, I will have to include it in the daily routine; in the car when stopped by a red light; asking You for a parking place; at the side of a sick friend; before each meal; just before I make that special telephone call; pausing right then to pray with a friend rather than just talking about his/her needs. So, Lord, help me to saturate my life with the lubricating oil of prayer.

Vitality

God's Word to Me

They shall still bring forth fruit in old age; they shall be full of sap [of spiritual vitality] and rich in the verdure [of trust, love and contentment].

Psalm 92:14, AMP

Children's children are the crown of old men, and the glory of children is their father.

Proverbs 17:6, NKJV

Prayer-Meditation

What a beautiful ideal for the golden years, Lord! I think with gratitude of _____ and _____ in our church fellowship, and of those of my own family in whom this promise is being so abundantly fulfilled. And I praise You that bearing fruit is not a matter of age but of the infusion of spiritual vitality from Your Spirit.

Protection

God's Word to Me

Put on the whole armor of God
... above all, taking the shield of
faith with which you will be able
to quench all the fiery darts of
the wicked one.

Ephesians 6:11, 16, NKJV

He will redeem my soul in peace
from the battle which is against
me, for they are many who strive
with me.

Psalm 55:18, NASB

Prayer-Meditation

Lord, I know from experience
that evil cannot be vanquished
by moral platitudes or ethical
ideals. I need an act of will even
more than of reason, and that is
what You mean by "faith." This
faith is not in myself, but in You,
Lord, making me sufficient for
everything. I now claim possession of this most important
weapon, which will become the
core of my defense.

Asking Prayer

God's Word to Me

So I tell you, whatever you pray
for and ask, believe you have got
it, and you shall have it.

Mark 11:24, MOFFATT

Your kingdom come, your will
be done on earth as it is in
heaven.

Matthew 6:10, NIV

Prayer-Meditation

Hope must be in the future
tense. Faith—to be faith—must
always be in the present tense.
Only faith will forgive sins, or
resist Satan, or heal. In the
Gospels we watch Jesus putting
into practice the principle given
us in Mark 11:24. Zacchaeus
had spent his life in sin. Yet
Jesus said, "*This* day is salvation
come to this house" (Luke 19:9).
The man at the pool of Bethesda
had been a cripple for thirty-
eight years. Yet Jesus told him to
pick up his mat and walk *now*
(John 5:8).

Lord, my prayer is, "May Thy
kingdom come for me in every
area of my life *now*."

Words of Faith

God's Word to Me

For by your words you will be justified, and by your words you will be condemned.

Matthew 12:37, RSV

Immediately Jesus reached out his hand and caught him. "You of little faith," he said, "why did you doubt?"

Matthew 14:31, NIV

Read James 1:6–8.

Prayer-Meditation

Lord, I see it! So often I have prayed with faith for a gift or blessing or healing, then have proceeded to cancel out my prayer with words of doubt and unbelief. Your Spirit would bid me use *words* of faith to strengthen and buttress and build faith. Help me with this, Lord.

Redemption

God's Word to Me

I have blotted out, like a thick cloud, your transgressions, and like a cloud, your sins. Return to Me, for I have redeemed you.

Isaiah 44:22, NKJV

Or do you not know that your body is the temple of the Holy Spirit who is in you, whom you have from God, and you are not your own? For you were bought at a price; therefore glorify God in your body and in your spirit, which are God's.

1 Corinthians 6:19–20, NKJV

Prayer-Meditation

I praise You for being a forgiving Lord. But I see that there is one condition: I must give up my sinful ways and return unto You. I do this now, Lord, and kneel again at Your feet. Take my life, make it and mold it as You will. Thank You for unburdening me of so great a weight.

Jesus, the Intercessor

God's Word to Me

Therefore He [Jesus] is also able to save to the uttermost those who come to God through Him, since He ever lives to make intercession for them.

Hebrews 7:25, NKJV

Yet even now the Witness to my innocence is there in heaven; my Advocate is there on high.

Job 16:19, TLB

Prayer-Meditation

O risen and glorified Lord, how great it is that You are the High Priest in the heavenly Kingdom, that You are my personal Advocate who will take my heartfelt prayer before the throne of the Father.

In the hour of trial,
    Jesus plead for me;
Lest by base denial,
    I depart from Thee:
When Thou seest me waver,
    With a look recall,
Nor for fear or favor,
    Suffer me to fall.

James Montgomery, 1834

Adventurous Prayer

God's Word to Me

Ask, and you will receive. . . . What do you want Me to do for you?

John 16:24; Mark 10:36, NKJV

One thing I asked of the LORD, that will I seek after: to live in the house of the LORD all the days of my life.

Psalm 27:4, NRSV

Prayer-Meditation

Praying is dangerous business.

Peter Marshall

I asked for patience, Lord, and You sent me the slowest cleaning woman I've ever had. I asked for love, and You sent a cross-grained relative to stay with us for a month. I asked for the gift of faith, and for a season You withdrew Your face from me, forcing me to walk in darkness, trusting You blindly.

What a sense of humor You have, Lord! Your message to me is: "From here on, My child, be sure you mean what you ask Me for."

Praise

God's Word to Me

My heart rejoices in the Lord; my horn is exalted in the Lord. I smile at my enemies, because I rejoice in Your salvation. There is none holy like the Lord, for there is none besides You, nor is there any rock like our God.

1 Samuel 2:1–2, NKJV

Delight yourself in the LORD and he will give you the desires of your heart.

Psalm 37:4, NIV

Prayer-Meditation

By faith, O Holy Spirit, allow me to move beyond the surface appearance of my circumstance to touch the loving hand of my heavenly Father. As I praise Him in everything, I know that He is showering me with the gift of Himself in whatever happens. I reach out to receive His loving kindness.

Repentance

God's Word to Me

Repent therefore, and turn again . . . that times of refreshing may come from the presence of the Lord.

Acts 3:19, RSV

As the deer pants for streams of water, so my soul pants for you, O God. My soul thirsts for God, for the living God.

Psalm 42:1–2, NIV

Read John 7:37–39.

Prayer-Meditation

Lord, I have been going through a time of spiritual barrenness, of boredom and arid unhappiness. Pleasures once enjoyed have gone stale. I am often tense and ill-humored. And You have seemed far away.

I repent of a certain enjoyment of this. I repent of the hardness of heart that is behind this inner distress. Lord, how I need the cool, refreshing gift of the Holy Spirit in my life! I open my heart now to receive Him.

Surrender of the Will

God's Word to Me

We all, like sheep, have gone astray, each of us has turned to his own way; and the Lord has laid on him the iniquity of us all.

Isaiah 53:6, NIV

Do not be conformed to this world, but be transformed by the renewing of your minds, so that you may discern what is the will of God—what is good and acceptable and perfect.

Romans 12:2, NRSV

Prayer-Meditation

In my blindness, Lord, I willed to have it my own way and ended up a lost person, simply having conformed to the crowd. Lord, I surrender my willfulness; give me Your willingness.

Spiritual Cleansing

God's Word to Me

He who has clean hands will be stronger and stronger.

Job 17:9, NKJV

Then He answered and spoke to those who stood before Him, saying, "Take away the filthy garments from him." And to him He said, "See, I have removed your iniquity from you, and I will clothe you with rich robes."

Zechariah 3:4, NKJV

Prayer-Meditation

Lord, my hands have been in filth too many times. Today I stretch them out to You for a spiritual scrubbing. I want to bathe totally in Your light so that every dirty place, both inside and out, is cleansed. Then when people look upon me, they will see me as You view me: cleansed completely through the blood of Jesus.

A Time for Silence

God's Word to Me

But He answered her not a word.

Matthew 15:23, NKJV

And you have forgotten the exhortation which is addressed to you as sons, "My son, do not regard lightly the discipline of the Lord, nor faint when you are reproved by Him; for those whom the Lord loves he disciplines, and He scourges every son whom He receives."

Hebrews 12:5–6, NASB

Prayer-Meditation

Lord Jesus, recently when I turned to You inwardly to ask how I should reply to someone, Your answer was, "Not a word." Then You reminded me of Your silences in the Gospels.

Lord, Your silences unsettle us, as they are meant to. How eloquently Your silence says, "You, My child, are out of order. Get back on track."

Practicing His Presence

God's Word to Me

They are not of the world, just as I am not of the world.

John 17:16, NKJV

Now when Daniel learned that the decree had been published, he went home to his upstairs room. . . . Three times a day he got down on his knees and prayed, giving thanks to his God, just as he had done before.

Daniel 6:10, NIV

Prayer-Meditation

Father, I know that by the word of Jesus I am not of the world. But sometimes I find myself caught up in such a schedule of activities that my prayer closet is empty. Then my disposition becomes irritable, critical, self-centered, and generally unhealthy.

Help me, Lord, to remember that my primary purpose is not to be involved in the world but to have unceasing fellowship with You, thereby becoming Your representative, Your hands and feet and voice in the world.

Purity

God's Word to Me

Blessed are the pure in heart, for they shall see God.

Matthew 5:8, NKJV

Who shall ascend the hill of the LORD? And who shall stand in his holy place? Those who have clean hands and pure hearts, who do not lift up their souls to what is false, and do not swear deceitfully.

Psalm 24:3–4, NRSV

Prayer-Meditation

What a tremendous promise! The question then arises, "Who could ever become pure in such a contaminated world?"

Yet, Lord, I think many of us have a deep hunger to be purified, to be clean so that we would be fit to stand in Your presence. The path is narrow, we face ridicule and scorn, and we need Your strength and support to make the journey.

Oh, Lord, I want so much to be with You. Help me.

Spiritual Warfare

God's Word to Me

He who sins is of the devil, for the devil has sinned from the beginning. For this purpose the Son of God was manifested, that He might destroy the works of the devil.

1 John 3:8, NKJV

The God of peace will soon crush Satan under your feet. The blessings from our Lord Jesus Christ be upon you.

Romans 16:20, TLB

Prayer-Meditation

Whenever I am attacked, oppressed, or tempted by the evil one, I can stand firm on this promise: Jesus has won the victory over Satan. I too can be victorious over the enemy by claiming the power in the Name of Jesus.

The Word

God's Word to Me

Your word I have hidden in my heart, that I might not sin against You.

Psalm 119:11, NKJV

Every Scripture is God-breathed —given by His inspiration—and profitable for instruction, for reproof and conviction of sin, for correction of error and discipline in obedience, and for training in righteousness [that is, in holy living, in conformity to God's will in thought, purpose and action].

2 Timothy 3:16, AMP

Prayer-Meditation

Hiding Your Word in my heart must mean memorizing many of the precious promises in the treasure chest of Scripture. When I meet that condition, then I have Your assurance, Lord, that the claiming of these promises will be a bulwark and protection for me. Help me to get on with it, Lord.

He Finishes His Work

God's Word to Me

He who has begun a good work in you will complete it until the day of Jesus Christ.

Philippians 1:6, NKJV

To him who is able to keep you from falling and to present you before his glorious presence without fault and with great joy—to the only God our Savior be glory, majesty, power and authority, through Jesus Christ our Lord, before all ages, now and forevermore! Amen.

Jude 24–25, NIV

Prayer-Meditation

It excites me, Lord, to know that when we invite You into our lives, this is only a beginning. You never let us go.

Christ's Prayer for His People

God's Word to Me

I have manifested Your name to the men whom You have given Me out of the world.

John 17:6, NKJV

But you were washed, but you were sanctified, but you were justified in the name of the Lord Jesus Christ, and in the Spirit of our God.

1 Corinthians 6:11b, NASB

Prayer-Meditation

How often, Jesus, I have heard the flip remark, "What's in a name anyway?" But it is obvious here that names are very important—for in Your prayer You personify the Name of God the Father to those who shared daily life with You.

To me, this means that in the handling of all my domestic relationships, attitudes toward work, pleasure, and people—as well as worship—I should manifest the God in me to others.

Come, Holy Spirit, infuse me anew!

The Humanity of Jesus

God's Word to Me

And now, O Father, glorify Me together with Yourself, with the glory which I had with You before the world was.

John 17:5, NKJV

But because of our sins he was wounded, beaten because of the evil we did. We are healed by the punishment he suffered, made whole by the blows he received.

Isaiah 53:5, TEV

Prayer-Meditation

This verse makes me realize the great cost to You, Jesus, in being born of a woman, in deliberately taking upon Yourself the limitations of finite man, in leaving Your heavenly glory to come to earth to be the door of reconciliation between man and God.

"Our God to earth come down!" How glorious! What cost!

Christ's Passion

God's Word to Me

Jesus spoke these words, lifted up His eyes to heaven, and said: "Father, the hour has come. Glorify Your Son, that Your Son also may glorify You."

John 17:1, NKJV

Prayer-Meditation

What a contrast this Scripture presents to my life! Jesus knew that the "hour of the Cross" had come. Yet He asked only for the Father's help in completing His sacrificial mission—the reason He had come to earth—that the Father would be glorified in the Son.

Lord, deliver me from expecting personal spiritual rewards or benefits from any service I render to You. Lift my eyes to the larger horizon of Your Kingdom and Your glory.

Christ's Sacrifice

God's Word to Me

Then He took the twelve aside and said unto them, "Behold, we are going up to Jerusalem, and all things that are written by the prophets concerning the Son of Man will be accomplished."

Luke 18:31, NKJV

From that time Jesus began to show to His disciples that He must go to Jerusalem, and suffer many things from the elders and chief priests and scribes, and be killed, and be raised again the third day.

Matthew 16:21, NKJV

Prayer-Meditation

Lord Jesus, thank You for this demonstration of obedience and courage. With all the agony of Gethsemane already in Your Spirit, You deliberately went forward. Help me to remember this, Lord, when I would flee from trouble.

The Listening Heart

God's Word to Me

And he said, "Who are You, Lord?"

Acts 9:5, NKJV

But they were hearing only, "He who formerly persecuted us now preaches the faith which he once tried to destroy."

Galatians 1:23, NKJV

Read Acts 7:58.

Prayer-Meditation

"Saul, Saul, why persecutest thou Me?" Jesus Christ knew his name! And in that question to him, Saul also recognized the voice of Jesus Christ. No wonder Saul trembled and fell on his face. His deeds, done in religious zeal, were being denounced by the living Lord. But Jesus loved this zealot and saw his enormous potential, even though He had to renounce Saul's works.

Lord, help me to listen first, that my works will not be in vain but a glory to Your Name.

My Prayer Requests

_____
_____
_____
_____
_____
_____
_____
_____
_____
_____

God's Answers

_____
_____
_____
_____
_____
_____
_____
_____
_____
_____

April

April 1

The Sovereignty of God

God's Word to Me

And the chief priests and the scribes sought how they might take Him by trickery and put Him to death. But they said, "Not during the feast, lest there be an uproar of the people."

Mark 14:1–2, NKJV

They were seeking therefore to seize Him; and no man laid his hand on Him, because His hour had not yet come.

John 7:30, NASB

Prayer-Meditation

Nothing more clearly shows Your total sovereignty, Father. The cunning of man could not move forward by one second Your timing for the sacrifice of Your Son. Lord, give me such faith in Your overruling sovereignty that I am delivered from concern about the reactions of people to anything I do. And create in me a holy awe that final power in heaven and on earth is still Yours.

April 2

Jesus, Our Paschal Sacrifice

God's Word to Me

But God chose what is foolish in the world to shame the wise, God chose what is weak in the world to shame the strong.

1 Corinthians 1:27, RSV

Purge (clean out) the old leaven that you may be fresh (new) dough, still uncontaminated (as you are), for Christ, our Passover [Lamb], has been sacrificed.

1 Corinthians 5:7, AMP

Prayer-Meditation

For the Israelites across long centuries, a helpless lamb was commanded by God to be their sacrifice for sin. And so, in the fulness of time, a baby, lying in the crook of a woman's arm, was in reality God tabernacling with men through that tiny body. He, the Child, as helpless as the lamb, would become our paschal sacrifice in order to reign as King of kings and Lord of lords.

74

Gethsemane

God's Word to Me

He [Jesus] said to them, "My soul is exceedingly sorrowful, even to death. Stay here and watch." And when He returned, He found them asleep again . . . and they did not know what to answer Him.

Mark 14:34, 40, NKJV

He is despised and rejected by men, a Man of sorrows and acquainted with grief. And we hid, as it were, our faces from Him; He was despised, and we did not esteem Him.

Isaiah 53:3, NKJV

Prayer-Meditation

Jesus, how often I have failed here. Because I could think of nothing to say in prayer, I have allowed my tired flesh to rule— sleeping instead of watching and waiting for You to speak to me. Strengthen my spirit, Lord, to rule my flesh.

Crowd Pressure

God's Word to Me

And all the people answered and said, "His blood be on us and on our children."

Matthew 27:25, NKJV

For the waywardness of the naive shall kill them, and the complacency of fools shall destroy them. But he who listens to me shall live securely, and shall be at ease from the dread of evil.

Proverbs 1:32–33, NASB

Prayer-Meditation

Lord, this Scripture has always horrified me by its stark truth. For I see all too clearly that well-intentioned people can become weak and heartless in a crowd situation. Forgive me for the times I have ignored You, denied You, failed You in order to be more acceptable to those around me. Help me, Lord, to have more courage and boldness in taking a stand for what is right.

Trust

God's Word to Me

Read Luke 24:13–35.

Those who trust in the LORD are like Mount Zion, which cannot be shaken but endures forever.

Psalm 125:1, NIV

Prayer-Meditation

The apostles had been with their master for three years: hearing His teaching, witnessing incredible miracles, feeling the impact of His personality. Yet now they were dejected men—"We had hoped . . . He promised to rise on the third day." In despair Peter grumbled, "It's no use. I'm going back to my old life—fishing."

Yet there was the risen Lord, walking beside the disciples on the road to Emmaus; standing on the beach waiting for Peter.

Open my eyes, Lord, to see that You and You alone can always be trusted, that You and You alone will always be a rock of dependability in a world of uncertainty.

The Resurrection

God's Word to Me

Jesus said to her, "I am the resurrection and the life. He who believes in me, though he may die, he shall live. And whoever lives and believes in Me shall never die. Do you believe this?"

John 11:25–26, NKJV

Read Luke 24:5; Romans 6:9–11.

Prayer-Meditation

Love's redeeming work is done, Alleluia!
Fought the fight, the battle won, Alleluia!
Vain the stone, the watch, the seal, Alleluia!
Christ has burst the gates of hell, Alleluia!

Charles Wesley

Thank You, Lord, for the magnificent promise that through our belief in You, we too will have a resurrection experience and life eternal. Do I fully understand the significance of this?

Faithfulness

God's Word to Me

Jesus said to her, "Mary!"

John 20:16, NKJV

Live by the Spirit, I say, and do not gratify the desires of the flesh.

Galatians 5:16, NRSV

Read John 10:11–17.

Prayer-Meditation

Jesus called her by name, and Mary knew Him even by the way He spoke her name! The surge of her emotions was such that she reached out to hug Him to herself. But even as the grave could not hold Him, neither could her love restrain Him. Instead, His love held her at full attention as she listened to His instructions and in immediate obedience went forth to fulfill them.

O Lord Jesus, help me to live in Your Spirit—not in my emotions.

Joy

God's Word to Me

Therefore you now have sorrow; but I will see you again and your heart will rejoice, and your joy no one will take from you.

John 16:22, NKJV

Let the trees in the woods sing for joy before the LORD, for he comes to judge the earth.

1 Chronicles 16:33, TLB

Prayer-Meditation

"Joy cometh in the morning." It's true, Lord! As I awaken to greet You with each new day, my heart springs with joy. As You impart Yourself to me, I find that circumstances of life can dim but never destroy the joy You have given me.

Renewal Time

God's Word to Me

For, lo, the winter is past.... The flowers appear on the earth; the time of the singing of birds is come.

Song of Solomon 2:11–12, KJV

And I will always guide you and satisfy you with good things. I will keep you strong and well. You will be like a garden that has plenty of water, like a spring of water that never goes dry.

Isaiah 58:11, TEV

Prayer-Meditation

Thank You, Father, for the steady renewal of life. During the long winter months when the limbs of trees are bare, I know that spring will come again, that sap will rise and fresh green leaves appear. Even so, thank You that I need not despair through days drab with seemingly unimportant tasks, through dark periods of waiting for prayers to be answered, through times when I am unable to feel Your presence. Thank You that Your life is always there. Praise You for spring!

Resurrection of Hope

God's Word to Me

Blessed be the God and Father of our Lord Jesus Christ, who according to His abundant mercy has begotten us again to a living hope through the resurrection of Jesus Christ from the dead.

1 Peter 1:3, NKJV

Peter, however, got up and ran to the tomb. Bending over, he saw the strips of linen lying by themselves, and he went away, wondering to himself what had happened.

Luke 24:12, NIV

Prayer-Meditation

Father, so many times I have felt bereft of all hope; in this I can relate to the disciples during the period between the crucifixion and resurrection of Jesus. So, thank You, Father, for Your great mercy in restoring our hope through the resurrection of Jesus Christ, Whom no grave could contain.

Persecution

God's Word to Me

Blessed are you when they revile and persecute you, and say all kinds of evil against you falsely for My sake.

Matthew 5:11, NKJV

For do I now persuade men, or God? Or do I seek to please men? For if I still pleased men, I would not be a servant of Christ.

Galatians 1:10, NKJV

Prayer-Meditation

Lord, there have been so many times when I've let myself be a "people pleaser" that I wince on reading these hard words. Deep down, I would give almost anything to be able to confront Your scoffers boldly and suffer humiliation for Your sake.

I pray for courage and total selflessness when the opportunity comes to be persecuted for Your sake.

Resurrection Appearances

God's Word to Me

So when they had eaten breakfast, Jesus said to Simon Peter, "Simon, son of Jonah, do you love Me . . . ?"

John 21:15, NKJV

Read Matthew 16:15–20; Romans 1:16.

Prayer-Meditation

There had been a day when Jesus had called him "Peter." Why? Because it was symbolic of the confession Simon had made when God revealed to him that the "rock" foundation of our faith is that Jesus Christ is the Son of God. But now, in this post-resurrection appearance, Jesus reverted to the family name to ask: What is your relationship with Me now, Simon? Do you love Me more than your own life? Are you prepared to confess Me as Christ and as Lord? Will you be Peter—or Simon?

Lord, help me fully and unashamedly to live in the name You have given to me—Christian.

Rejoicing

God's Word to Me

And it will be said in that day: "Behold, this is our God; we have waited for Him, and He will save us. . . . We will be glad and rejoice in His salvation."

Isaiah 25:9, NKJV

Then my soul shall rejoice in the LORD, exulting in his deliverance.

Psalm 35:9, NRSV

Prayer-Meditation

O Lord, open our understanding so that we will not be as those who heard or read the promise of Your coming, yet never believed. Help us to rejoice in Your salvation which has become the salvation of all who truly believe You and confess, "Yes, Jesus is *my* Savior."

Resurrection Promise

God's Word to Me

And the graves were opened; and many bodies of the saints who had fallen asleep were raised.

Matthew 27:52, NKJV

Where, O death, is your victory? Where, O death, is your sting?

1 Corinthians 15:55, NIV

Prayer-Meditation

Jesus, when You conquered death, what hope You gave to all of us! "O grave, where is thy victory, O death, where is thy sting?" This verse above confirms to me, Lord, that if I "die in Christ" I will surely rise to reign with You.

Your Reservation with Jesus

God's Word to Me

To an inheritance incorruptible and undefiled and that does not fade away, reserved in heaven for you.

1 Peter 1:4, NKJV

And if we are [His] children, then we are [His] heirs also: heirs of God and fellow heirs with Christ—sharing His inheritance with Him; only we must share His suffering if we are to share His glory.

Romans 8:17, AMP

Prayer-Meditation

Our future reservations have already been made in heaven where, as children of God, we are promised to be "fellow heirs with Christ" (Romans 8:17). But as Jesus suffered while on earth, we are fellow heirs with Him here too in facing opposition, persecution, unbelief!

Lord, keep me mindful that as a fellow heir with You, all the power of heaven is available to me here and now to keep that which You have won for me.

The Transfiguration

God's Word to Me

And [Jesus] was transfigured before them. His face shone like the sun, and His clothes became as white as the light. And behold, Moses and Elijah appeared to them, talking with Him.

Matthew 17:2–3, NKJV

And the Word became flesh and dwelt among us, and we beheld His glory, the glory as of the only begotten of the Father, full of grace and truth.

John 1:14, NKJV

Prayer-Meditation

Lord Jesus, what an incredible experience for those disciples to have been *there* with You, Moses, and Elijah! I pray that as Your disciple today I will know the joy of conversation with You, the excitement of feeling Your presence in my life, and the thrill of taking Your fresh concepts and ideas and putting them to work in my life.

Faith

God's Word to Me

Then a voice came from heaven. . . . The crowd standing by heard it and said that it had thundered.

John 12:28–29, RSV

Beware then of your own hearts, dear brothers, lest you find that they, too, are evil and unbelieving and are leading you away from the living God.

Hebrews 3:12, TLB

Prayer-Meditation

I am discovering, Lord, that in every answer to prayer, every modern miracle of guidance or healing or changed lives, You still always leave room for the unbelief of those who say, "Oh, only coincidence," or, "It's only thunder."

Thank You for alerting us to expect this stubborn unbelief (Luke 16:31) so that our faith will not be shaken nor our praise diminished by it.

Obedience

God's Word to Me

I can of Myself do nothing. As I hear, I judge; and My judgment is righteous, because I do not seek My own will but the will of the Father who sent Me.

John 5:30, NKJV

You in Your mercy have led forth the people whom You have redeemed; You have guided them in Your strength to Your holy habitation.

Exodus 15:13, NKJV

Prayer-Meditation

"As I hear" . . . I must stop and really listen to You, Lord, then let my decision arise from what You say to me. Lord, I do want to follow You. Yet often I have excused my self-will by saying that Your will has not been clear. Help me today to obey You unquestioningly and immediately, leaving the results to You.

Worship

God's Word to Me

Now it came to pass in those days that He went out to the mountain to pray, and continued all night in prayer to God.

Luke 6:12, NKJV

The land produced vegetation: plants bearing seed according to their kinds and trees bearing fruit with seed in it according to their kinds. And God saw that it was good.

Genesis 1:12, NIV

Prayer-Meditation

Jesus loved the out-of-doors: He prayed as the sun rose; He chose a hillside or lakeside for teaching; a boat pushed from shore suited Him for a pulpit; the Garden of Gethsemane for a climactic confrontation.

Lord, help me discover the healing of nature to my spirit. For the peace and hush of the forests, the vastness of the sea, the grandeur of the mountains, the delicate beauty of flowers, I praise You. The heavens do indeed declare Your glory, the earth Your love.

Protection

God's Word to Me

Indeed before the day was, I am He; and there is no one who can deliver out of My hand.

Isaiah 43:13, NKJV

My sheep hear My voice, and I know them, and they follow Me. And I give them eternal life, and they shall never perish; neither shall anyone snatch them out of My hand.

John 10:27–28, NKJV

Prayer-Meditation

Thank You, O loving Father, for this wonderful promise! Here I find confidence that even when I am weak and faltering, because I have committed my life to You, no one—no evil power—can "pluck" me out of Your hand. You have accepted full responsibility for keeping me for Yourself.

Spiritual Warfare

God's Word to Me

You will keep him in perfect peace, whose mind [imagination] is stayed on You.

Isaiah 26:3, NKJV

The LORD is my light and my salvation; whom shall I fear? The LORD is the stronghold of my life; of whom shall I be afraid?

Psalm 27:1, NRSV

Prayer-Meditation

I know, Lord, that one of the places Satan gets to me is through my imagination. In every circumstance, he can present, "What if?" followed by negative pictures. Or he will infiltrate my thinking with a sordid image.

I now hand my imagination over to You, asking that you purify it, baptize it, possess it. Then I will confront Satan, saying, "You have no ground in me anymore."

New Life

God's Word to Me

Sing to God, sing praises to His name; cast up a highway for Him who rides through the deserts; His name is the Lord, be in high spirits and glory before Him!

Psalm 68:4, AMP

Prayer-Meditation

It's spring, Lord. The earth is very beautiful, and my heart is singing. This morning I saw Your handiwork in the beauty of masses of rhododendron. What consummate artistry!

I heard Your voice in a child's bubbling laughter. I felt Your tender compassion as a baby robin fell out of the nest and had to be rescued.

Thank You for eyes to appreciate the beauty You have made, for a spirit to stand on tiptoe and worship You.

Cleanse My Thoughts

God's Word to Me

It is written, "My house is a house of prayer," but you have made it a "den of thieves."

Luke 19:46, NKJV

Search me, O God, and know my heart; test me and know my thoughts. See if there is any wicked way in me, and lead me in the way everlasting.

Psalm 139:23–24, NRSV

Read Isaiah 56:7; Jeremiah 7:11.

Prayer-Meditation

Father, as I reflect on this Scripture, I realize that I have often allowed the thieving thoughts of my cares and concerns to rob both You and me of our time for precious dialogue. I commit all my thoughts to You that You may sift out the chaff and gather the grain.

God's Rest

God's Word to Me

Come to Me, all you who labor and are heavy laden, and I will give you rest.

Matthew 11:28, NKJV

Seeing then that we have a great High Priest who has passed through the heavens, Jesus the Son of God, let us hold fast our confession.

Hebrews 4:14, NKJV

Read Matthew 11:29–30.

Prayer-Meditation

How often I return to these words, Lord! For the world of today seems to get more and more turbulent, not less. When worry takes over and self-pity consumes me, I go off by myself and seek to lose myself in You.

When my body, mind, and spirit are one in You, then comes Your blessed rest.

Joy

God's Word to Me

"The joy of the Lord is your strength." . . . And all the people went their way to eat and drink . . . and rejoice greatly, because they understood.

Nehemiah 8:10, 12, NKJV

Make haste, my beloved, and be like a gazelle or a young stag upon the mountains of spices!

Song of Solomon 8:14, NRSV

Prayer-Meditation

Slow me down, Lord, and let me enjoy Your world today. I fear that I have been too deadly serious, too intent, even too religious. I want to laugh, to take delight in a member of my family, to be romantic for a moment, to have some fun! It will be a gift from You I'd like to enjoy for the sheer pleasure of it.

God's Call

God's Word to Me

I saw the Lord sitting on a throne, high and lifted up, and the train of His robe filled the temple.

Isaiah 6:1, NKJV

After these things the word of the LORD came to Abram in a vision, saying, "Do not be afraid, Abram. I am your shield, your exceedingly great reward."

Genesis 15:1, NKJV

Prayer-Meditation

Isaiah, an ordinary businessman of his day, was in the temple, worshiping the Lord, as was his custom. God had a job to get done and He needed a dependable human being. God saw Isaiah's heart at worship and asked, "Whom shall I send?" Isaiah caught the vision and answered, "Here am I, send me."

O God, help me keep my heart fixed on You that I may hear Your voice and be open to a vision of the heavenlies!

Love

God's Word to Me

A sower went out to sow . . . some seeds fell by the roadside, and the birds came and ate them up.

Matthew 13:3–4, AMP

See how great a love the Father has bestowed upon us, that we should be called children of God; and such we are. For this reason the world does not know us, because it did not know Him.

1 John 3:1, NASB

Prayer-Meditation

Lord, I am overwhelmed with the extravagance of Your love! For like the sower in Your parable, You never looked back to see where the seed of Your ministry was falling. You knew that where it was received, it would bear fruit of its own kind.

Thank You, Holy Spirit, for preparing my heart to receive the seeds of such a lavish love.

Truth through His Word

God's Word to Me

Sanctify them by Your truth. Your word is truth.

John 17:17, NKJV

Do not snatch the word of truth from my mouth, for I have put my hope in your laws.

Psalm 119:43, NIV

Prayer-Meditation

It is wonderful, Lord, how a long season of frustration and doubt can suddenly be dispelled by something I catch in Your Word. As You trim away the unimportant and the superfluous, I pray that You will give me Your perspective and bring Jesus clearly into view. In this way the answer to a troublesome situation will seem so simple!

Continue, Father, to purify my thoughts by feeding in Your truth so that my actions will flow out of simple obedience into sanctifying power and blessing for others.

Bread of Life

God's Word to Me

And Jesus said to them, "I am the bread of life. He who comes to Me shall never hunger, and he who believes in Me shall never thirst."

John 6:35, NKJV

He got up, and ate and drank; then he went in the strength of that food forty days and forty nights to Horeb the mount of God.

1 Kings 19:8, NRSV

Prayer-Meditation

Lord, this morning I was hungry in my spirit and Your Word fed me. I had a thirst for righteousness (evil and deception are all about), and You came to me. The purity of Your Presence cleansed me.

Lord Jesus, You are indeed the bread of life.

Love That Lasts

God's Word to Me

Who shall separate us from the love of Christ? Shall tribulation, or distress, or persecution, or famine, or nakedness, or peril, or sword? . . . No . . . .

Romans 8:35, 37, RSV

For I am convinced that nothing can separate us from his love. Death can't, and life can't. The angels won't, and all the powers of hell itself cannot keep God's love away . . . . nothing will ever be able to separate us from the love of God.

Romans 8:38–39, TLB

Prayer-Meditation

O Love that will not let me go.

George Matheson

We have been captured by You, O Lord, and are held so tightly that nothing will be able to wrest us from Your hand.

I keep this promise before me in times of sickness and discouragement and when tempted by the world. Your love overcomes all.

My Prayer Requests

_____

_____

_____

_____

_____

_____

_____

_____

_____

God's Answers

_____

_____

_____

_____

_____

_____

_____

_____

_____

May

Joyous Expectancy

God's Word to Me

Unless you are converted and become as little children, you will by no means enter the kingdom of heaven.

Matthew 18:3, NKJV

"Dear woman, why do you involve me?" Jesus replied. "My time has not yet come." His mother said to the servants, "Do whatever he tells you."

John 2:4–5, NIV

Prayer-Meditation

Spiritual life is the life of a child. . . . Certainty is the mark of the common-sense life; gracious uncertainty is the mark of the spiritual life. . . . We are not uncertain of God, but uncertain of what He is going to do next. . . . Thus life is full of spontaneous, joyful uncertainty and expectancy.

Oswald Chambers

Adventurous Living

God's Word to Me

I will bring the blind by a way they did not know; I will lead them in paths they have not known.

Isaiah 42:16, NKJV

Since we have such [glorious] hope—such [joyful and confident] expectation—we speak very freely and openly and fearlessly.

2 Corinthians 3:12, AMP

Prayer-Meditation

Thank You, Lord, for the promise of a suspenseful, adventurous life when we follow Your guidance. I ask for the gift of a listening heart to hear Your voice and the gift of boldness to follow through on any marching orders You give me.

Loneliness

God's Word to Me

Delight yourself also in the Lord, and He shall give you the desires of your heart.

Psalm 37:4, NKJV

Then the LORD God said, "It is not good for the man to be alone; I will make him a helper suitable for him."

Genesis 2:18, NASB

Prayer-Meditation

Lord, You are dearer to me than a whole company of people; You are my Friend. I rejoice in the life we share together. But when You looked upon Adam, You said it was not good that man should be alone, and You gave him Eve. Father, I too long for a human companion with whom to share dreams and meaningful experiences. I entrust this desire to You.

A Listening Heart

God's Word to Me

Jesus saith unto her, Said I not unto thee, that, if thou wouldest believe, thou shouldest see the glory of God?

John 11:40, KJV

Jesus said to her, "I am the resurrection and the life. He who believes in me will live, even though he dies; and whoever lives and believes in me will never die. Do you believe this?"

John 11:25–26, NIV

Read John 1:1–45.

Prayer-Meditation

Martha had confessed Him with her own mouth: "Thou art the Christ, the Son of God." But she had not been really listening to His words when He asked, "Believest thou this . . . whosoever liveth and believeth in Me shall never die?" Even Mary, who had sat at His feet, who had anointed His head, did not really hear Him.

Lord, help me to cultivate a listening heart so that when You speak to me, I will have ears to hear You.

Conversation with God

God's Word to Me

And there appeared to them Elijah with Moses; and they were talking to Jesus.

Mark 9:4, RSV

Then a cloud appeared and covered them with its shadow, and a voice came from the cloud, "This is my own dear Son—listen to him!"

Mark 9:7, TEV

Prayer-Meditation

As Jesus gave Peter, James, and John the privilege of listening to His conversation with Moses and Elijah, so God likes to share Himself with us. In fact, He wants to give each one of us a vision that will prepare us for the future. But like Peter, we tend to be uncomfortable in the presence of the almighty God, and we interrupt Him—robbing ourselves.

Father, so often my busy mind keeps darting ahead in every conversation I have with people—and You. Help me to keep still and really listen to the quiet voice of Jesus' Spirit within.

Selflessness

God's Word to Me

We have renounced the hidden things of shame, not walking in craftiness nor handling the word of God deceitfully, but by manifestation of the truth commending ourselves to every man's conscience in the sight of God.

2 Corinthians 4:2, NKJV

Speak out, judge righteously, defend the rights of the poor and needy.

Proverbs 31:9, NRSV

Prayer-Meditation

Father, do I rightly understand this verse in Paul's letter to the Corinthians to mean not to approach every situation and opportunity with, "What's in it for me"; or always manipulating people to my desired ends?

Lord, I pray for the negotiators of labor disputes, for legislators in every phase of our government—for all who have responsibility to and for people—that they will not walk in craftiness, but walk in Your light.

Praise

God's Word to Me

While I live I will praise the Lord;
I will sing praises to my God
while I have my being.

Psalm 146:2, NKJV

Therefore, do not worry about tomorrow, for tomorrow will worry about its own things. Sufficient for the day is its own trouble.

Matthew 6:34, NKJV

Prayer-Meditation

Forgive me, Lord, when I am too eager for tomorrow to appreciate today. Forgive me when I'm too upset about yesterday to see that this day—when I praise You with all my heart—is indeed a beautiful new day.

Trust for Tomorrow

God's Word to Me

Are not five sparrows sold for two pennies? And not one of them is forgotten before God. . . . Fear not; you are of more value than many sparrows.

Luke 12:6–7, RSV

Read Matthew 6:24–34; James 4:14–15.

Prayer-Meditation

Said the robin to the sparrow,
　"I should really like to know
Why these anxious human
　beings rush about and
　worry so."
Said the sparrow to the robin,
　"Friend, I think that it must
　be
That they have no heavenly
　Father such as cares for you
　and me."

Elizabeth Cheney

Lord, I can see that I am the one trying to be "spiritual," while You are the practical One. This day I put my troubles into Your capable hands and trust You for tomorrow.

Challenge to Parents

God's Word to Me

Therefore you shall lay up these words of mine in your heart and in your soul. . . . You shall teach them to your children, speaking of them when you sit in your house, when you walk by the way, when you lie down, and when you rise up.

Deuteronomy 11:18–19, NKJV

Read 1 Corinthians 3:10–15.

Prayer-Meditation

What a sobering thought that our parenthood is part of our "works" that will go through the fire of Your judgment. As I teach my children Your commandments, I lay ten foundation pieces into the fabric of their lives. And the result of my obedience is that You will be a sovereign Lord over them. How much they need You in these times!

Challenge to Children

God's Word to Me

Now therefore, listen to me, my children, for blessed are those who keep my ways.

Proverbs 8:32, NKJV

He lets me rest in fields of green grass and leads me to quiet pools of fresh water. He gives me new strength. He guides me in the right paths, as he has promised.

Psalm 23:2–3, TEV

Prayer-Meditation

Is there anything more beautiful, Lord, than to see children and young people opening their hearts to You? You gave them a challenge nearly two thousand years ago when you looked deep into their eyes and said, "Follow Me." There is a cost, of course—"Keep My ways." It can mean ridicule, even rejection by the world. But oh, how You love them and bless them!

Mother, I Love You

God's Word to Me

Who can find a virtuous woman? for her price is far above rubies. . . . Strength and honour are her clothing. . . . In her tongue is the law of kindness. . . . Her children arise up, and call her blessed.

Proverbs 31:10, 25, 26, 28, KJV

Prayer-Meditation

Father, we would thank You today for our mothers who gave us life, who surrounded us early and late with love and care, whose prayers on our behalf still cling around the Throne of Grace, a haunting perfume of love's petitions. . . .

We know that no sentimentality on any one day, no material gifts, can atone for our neglect during the rest of the year.

So in the days ahead, may our love speak to the hearts who know love best—by kindness, compassion, simple courtesy, daily thoughtfulness.

Bless my mother, Lord, with Your benediction.

Peter Marshall

God the Matchmaker

God's Word to Me

Delight yourself also in the Lord, and He will give you the desires and secret petitions of your heart.

Psalm 37:4, AMP

If you then, who are evil, know how to give good gifts to your children, how much more will your Father in heaven give good things to those who ask him!

Matthew 7:11, NRSV

Prayer-Meditation

Lord, I do have a secret petition today, a deep desire of the heart. I ask that You lead our children (grandchildren) to the marriage partners of Your choice and that You, Lord, overrule our children, if necessary, in these crucial decisions.

And wherever these future members of our family are now, I ask You to bless them, to lead them to know You as their Lord, to protect and guide them. I thank You in advance for the answer to this prayer.

Persistent Prayer

God's Word to Me

God forbid that I should sin against the Lord in ceasing to pray for you.

1 Samuel 12:23, KJV

And pray in the Spirit on all occasions with all kinds of prayers and requests. With this in mind, be alert and always keep on praying for all the saints.

Ephesians 6:18, NIV

Read 1 Thessalonians 5:17.

Prayer-Meditation

These verses startle me, Lord. I have stopped praying for a person in need because I got weary, or was annoyed at the lack of results, or simply because I forgot. I see now that You take our commitments to pray for others so seriously that to fail to pray is actually a sin of omission.

Abortion

God's Word to Me

Jesus said, "You shall not kill ...."

Matthew 19:18, RSV

Read Psalm 139:13.

Prayer-Meditation

Lord, I would talk to You this morning about a particular young woman. She has a difficult decison to make. Will she follow millions of her sisters and kill her unborn child by an abortion?

You alone can create life, Lord. We cannot. And all life is very precious to You. There stands Your immovable commandment that to kill Your creation is to sin against the Creator Himself.

Lord, give young women Your inner buttressing to see that "the way out is the way through." And show the rest of us how we can pray for those women who have had abortions, as well as for those who are making the decison this very day.

Adoration

God's Word to Me

Jesus said to her, "Do not cling to Me, for I have not yet ascended to My Father."

John 20:17, NKJV

Therefore, since we are receiving a kingdom that cannot be shaken, let us be thankful, and so worship God acceptably with reverence and awe, for our "God is a consuming fire."

Hebrews 12:28–29, NIV

Prayer-Meditation

O Lord, keep this teaching in my heart so that I would not be guilty of handling with familiarity that which is sacred. Through Jesus, I know that an audience with You, Father, can be warm and friendly, that You love each one of Your creations. But help me always to keep the right perspective so that You are always "very God of very God."

Wilderness Experience

God's Word to Me

Take heed lest you forget the Lord your God . . . who led you through the great and terrible wilderness . . . that he might humble you and test you, to do you good in the end.

Deuteronomy 8:11, 15–16, RSV

Prayer-Meditation

I am discovering, Father, that every life You intend to use mightily in Your service has a wilderness experience. The Israelites did. Jesus did (Luke 4:1–12). Saul of Tarsus did (Galatians 1:15–18).

A wilderness experience can be a time of struggle, of disappointment, of prayers seemingly unanswered—such as with a long illness—or being forcibly separated from those we love, or a period of helplessness through unemployment.

Help me, Father, to make my wilderness experience a time of growth, of learning, of spiritual maturation—and to understand that I could not handle the land flowing with milk and honey without going through this testing period.

New Direction

God's Word to Me

Behold, I am doing a new thing; now it springs forth; do you not perceive and know it, and will you not give heed to it? I will even make a way in the wilderness and rivers in the desert.

Isaiah 43:19, AMP

So I say to you, Ask, and it will be given you; search, and you will find; knock, and the door will be opened for you.

Luke 11:9, NRSV

Prayer-Meditation

Once our lives are planted in the grace of God, inevitably He is going to lead us out into new, untried paths, for that is the way of faith. That is the way of growth.

Lord, when I see a door closing behind me, let me not be fearful. Your promise is sure: You *will* open another door, making a way for me in what looks like an impossible wilderness. Thank You for the power that turns deserts into rivers of blessing.

Security

God's Word to Me

The Lord also will be a refuge for the oppressed, a refuge in times of trouble.

Psalm 9:9, NKJV

Yea, though I walk through the valley of the shadow of death, I will fear no evil; for You are with me; Your rod and Your staff, they comfort me.

Psalm 23:4, NKJV

Read Matthew 23:37.

Prayer-Meditation

Rock of Ages, cleft for me,
Let me hide myself in Thee.

Augustus M. Toplady

O Lord, Thou Guardian of my soul, walk before me through the dark shadows. Be a hiding place of safety for me. What security to be nestled in a crevice of the Rock which You are!

May 19

Spiritual Warfare

God's Word to Me

Take no part in the unfruitful works of darkness, but instead expose them.

Ephesians 5:11, RSV

I will give you the keys of the Kingdom of heaven; what you prohibit on earth will be prohibited in heaven, and what you permit on earth will be permitted in heaven.

Matthew 16:19, TEV

Prayer-Meditation

I do not consider myself to be a crusader, Lord. But I know that it is Your plan to use every disciple as a warrior against the forces of evil that surround us. Lord, I am willing to be used. My prayer now is that You will give me the gift of wisdom to know what evil works I am to expose, how to expose them, and to whom. Then give me loving words that carry the cutting edge of Your truth.

May 20

The Power of Agreement

God's Word to Me

Again I say to you, if two of you agree on earth about anything they ask, it will be done for them by my Father in heaven.

Matthew 18:19, RSV

Read Mark 5:40.

Prayer-Meditation

We notice, Lord, that in the case of Jairus' daughter, You permitted only the girl's parents and Peter, James, and John in the room. Jairus had already shown his faith by sending for the Master. You wanted only those in the room who agreed in faith.

This reminds us of our prayer-warrior friend, who is having the power of faith-agreement proved over and over. She also is finding that especially in prayers for healing, it is better to exclude those who cannot "agree."

Thank You, Lord, for teaching us this powerful principle of answered prayer.

Criticism

God's Word to Me

So do not criticize at all ... rather make up your mind never to put any stumbling-block or hindrance in your brother's way.

1 Corinthians 4:5;
Romans 14:13, MOFFATT

Love does not delight in evil but rejoices with the truth. It always protects, always trusts, always hopes, always perseveres.

1 Corinthians 13:6–7, NIV

Prayer-Meditation

Lord, since You told us that You came not to condemn us but to save us, who am I to be condemning and critical of others? Lord, cleanse me of the sin of this negative mind-set. Instead, let my concern of discernment or evaluation of others flow only into prayers for them.

Adoration

God's Word to Me

And when I saw Him, I fell at His feet as dead. But He laid His right hand on me, saying to me, "Do not be afraid; I am the First and the Last."

Revelation 1:17, NKJV

For it is written: "As I live, says the LORD, every knee shall bow to Me, and every tongue shall confess to God."

Romans 14:11, NKJV

Prayer-Meditation

Lord Jesus, how often I have longed to see You and adore You face-to-face! Yet this verse in Revelation shows how starkly my unclean self would be exposed if Your light shone on my mortal body. Even after so many years of growth in the faith, John prostrated himself before You with as much awe and fear as at Your resurrection. Teach us, Lord, how to worship You on earth as a preparation for that indescribable meeting in heaven.

Temptation

God's Word to Me

But you are those who have continued with Me in My trials.

Luke 22:28, NKJV

Read Luke 22:14–30.

Prayer-Meditation

Did you think temptations would end when you became a believer? When you were baptized in His Holy Spirit? The devil left Jesus only for a season; his harassment of the Son of man continued even to the cross. How then did Jesus live without sin? By staying in constant communication with His Father and obeying God's every instruction.

Take time to be holy,
     Speak oft' with thy Lord;
Abide in Him always
     And feed on His Word.

W. D. Longstaff

Lord, as You have instructed us, let my life be lived in constant dialogue with You and surrender to You.

Obedience

God's Word to Me

For we who live are always delivered to death for Jesus' sake, that the life of Jesus also may be manifested in our mortal flesh.

2 Corinthians 4:11, NKJV

Be careful to obey all these regulations I am giving you, so that it may always go well with you and your children after you, because you will be doing what is good and right in the eyes of the LORD your God.

Deuteronomy 12:28, NIV

Prayer-Meditation

Lord, every time I become conscious of sin in me, I suffer "death." For I find with Paul that my spirit longs to be totally submissive unto You. Yet I am grieved to find sin still active within me. Lord, continue in me Your work of cleansing, that Your resurrection life will be the life manifested in me.

Lifting Burdens

God's Word to Me

Blessed be the Lord, Who bears our burdens and carries us day by day, even the God Who is our salvation!

Psalm 68:19, AMP

I will refresh the weary and satisfy the faint.

Jeremiah 31:25, NIV

Prayer-Meditation

Lord Jesus, how marvelous that You came to earth to be our burden-bearer; that when I struggle along trying to carry my own burdens, I am actually usurping Your role.

How well You already know my present load, Lord. With joy, I roll these burdens onto Your shoulders, rejoicing that You are indeed my salvation.

Overcoming Trouble

God's Word to Me

In the world ye shall have tribulation: but be of good cheer; I have overcome the world.

John 16:33, KJV

It is the LORD who goes before you. He will be with you; he will not fail you or forsake you. Do not fear or be dismayed.

Deuteronomy 31:8, NRSV

Prayer-Meditation

Our Lord was always clear-eyed. In His last intimate talk with His apostles before His betrayal, He promised them— and us—troubles, problems, "tribulations." It must be so, simply because we are in the world where man's self-loving sin makes so much go awry.

But "cheer up," He assures us, "I will never leave you or forsake you. And I have put all this world of troubles under My feet."

Witnessing

God's Word to Me

All Scripture is God-breathed and is useful for teaching, rebuking, correcting and training in righteousness, so that the man of God may be thoroughly equipped for every good work.

2 Timothy 3:16–17, NIV

And my speech and my preaching were not with persuasive words of human wisdom, but in demonstration of the Spirit and of power, that your faith should not be in the wisdom of men but in the power of God.

1 Corinthians 2:4–5, NKJV

Prayer-Meditation

I confess, Lord, that like many Christians, when witnessing to others, I too often have ministered my own opinions rather than the Word. As I read Scripture each day, I pray that Your Word will permeate my being, and when I talk to spiritually hungry people, that Your Holy Spirit will speak through me with the words You want me to say.

Intercession for Believers

God's Word to Me

I do not pray for the world but for those whom You have given Me, for they are Yours.

John 17:9, NKJV

I pray that the God of our Lord Jesus Christ, the Father of glory, may give you a Spirit of wisdom and revelation as you come to know him.

Ephesians 1:17, NRSV

Prayer-Meditation

Lord Jesus, here You are giving me a sorely needed insight about prayer: I have spent too much time talking with You about those persons who steadfastly reject You and not enough time praying for those who love You and are committed to You. How reassuring that You, Lord, never cease to pray for those of us whom the Father has given You. Help me also to remember my responsibility to hold those believers in You in prayerful intercession.

God as Spirit

God's Word to Me

God is Spirit.

John 4:24, NKJV

No one has ever seen God. The only Son, who is the same as God and is at the Father's side, he has made him known.

John 1:18, TEV

Prayer-Meditation

Since God is Spirit, the world around us is filled with His presence. To the extent to which the ego, the "old man" in us, is put to death, God as Spirit can fill our minds and bodies and live in us, literally making us new creatures.

What an exciting truth, Father! I know that the very air I breathe is full of Your Spirit. This morning I open the door of my mind, my heart, my body to You and invite You to come in!

Prayer for a Sinner

God's Word to Me

If anyone sees his brother sinning a sin which does not lead to death, he will ask, and He [God] will give him life.

1 John 5:16, NKJV

Bear one another's burdens, and in this way you will fulfill the law of Christ.

Galatians 6:2, NRSV

Prayer-Meditation

Lord, I have needed this word on how to pray about someone who has been fleeing from You. What amazing authority You have given us, Your people! What a privilege that You bid me pray with the knowledge that You will find the way to restore and forgive and give this person new life.

Love

God's Word to Me

If I have all faith, so as to remove mountains, but have not love, I am nothing.

1 Corinthians 13:2, RSV

Little children, let us stop just saying we love people; let us really love them, and show it by our actions.

1 John 3:18, TLB

Prayer-Meditation

My heart an altar, and Thy love the flame.

George Croly

Accompany me today, O Spirit invisible, in all my goings, but stay with me also when I am in my own home and among my kindred.... Forbid that I should refuse to my own household the courtesy and politeness which I show strangers. Let charity today begin at home.

John Baillie

My Prayer Requests

_____

_____

_____

_____

_____

_____

_____

_____

_____

God's Answers

_____

_____

_____

_____

_____

_____

_____

_____

_____

_____

June

The New Creature

God's Word to Me

Therefore, if anyone is in Christ, he is a new creation; old things have passed away; behold, all things have become new.

2 Corinthians 5:17, NKJV

Therefore we have been buried with him by baptism into death . . . so we too might walk in newness of life.

Romans 6:4, NRSV

Prayer-Meditation

I know, Father, that I must come to You just as I am. But I also know that I dare not go away just as I came. . . .

Where I am blind, give me sight.
Where I fail to hear Your voice, please do something about my deafness.
Even where I deliberately choose to do what I know is wrong, You alone can change my divided will.
For, Lord, I acknowledge my total dependence upon You.

Peter Marshall

Jesus, Our Advocate

God's Word to Me

For Christ is not entered into the holy places made with hands . . . but into heaven itself, now to appear in the presence of God for us.

Hebrews 9:24, KJV

For there is one God and one mediator between God and men, the man Christ Jesus.

1 Timothy 2:5, NIV

Prayer-Meditation

What a high privilege to have Jesus Christ as my Advocate to mediate for me personally! I accept the responsibility this entails.

Lord, help me to provide You with an honest witness which You may use to present my case to the Supreme High Court of God.

Jesus, the Glorified Lord

God's Word to Me

[Jesus] has gone into heaven and is at the right hand of God, angels and authorities and powers having been made subject to Him.

1 Peter 3:22, NKJV

I am the Living One; I was dead, and behold I am alive for ever and ever! And I hold the keys of death and Hades.

Revelation 1:18, NIV

Read Hebrews 7:25–28.

Prayer-Meditation

Lord, help me to remember this Scripture and to stand rock-firm on it when I'm feeling wounded, confused, and needy. Help me also to remember that my glorified Lord is also my personal Friend and Savior. He knows me and He loves me.

Pursue Peace

God's Word to Me

He who would love life and see good days . . . let him seek peace and pursue it.

1 Peter 3:10–11, NKJV

Don't quarrel with anyone. Be at peace with everyone, just as much as possible.

Romans 12:18, TLB

Read Psalm 34:12–16.

Prayer-Meditation

Lord, I see something in this Scripture that convicts me. I have been so discouraged about world peace ever becoming a reality that I stopped praying for it. Wrong, of course.

But the words "seek" and "pursue" go beyond prayer. I am to take action. How? By living peace in my own life. I see now that one person's peaceful demeanor can become contagious.

Lord, let world peace begin with me.

Walk in the Spirit

God's Word to Me

For ye were sometimes darkness, but now are ye light in the Lord: walk as children of light.

Ephesians 5:8, KJV

And it came about that while He was in one of the cities, behold there was a man full of leprosy; and when he saw Jesus, he fell on his face and implored Him, saying, "Lord, if You are willing, You can make me clean."

Luke 5:12, NASB

Prayer-Meditation

I want to be Your "child of light," Lord, for there has been so much darkness in my life. I want my daily walk to bring others to an awareness of You. I pray that the luminescence of Your Spirit will flood through me, cleansing and eradicating every unclean spot or stain so that my body can be a temple of the Holy Spirit.

Heart Attitude

God's Word to Me

Therefore, as the Holy Spirit says: "Today, if you will hear His voice, do not harden your hearts as in the rebellion, in the day of trial in the wilderness."

Hebrews 3:7–8, NKJV

Moses heard the people of every family wailing, each at the entrance to his tent. The LORD became exceedingly angry, and Moses was troubled.

Numbers 11:10, NIV

Prayer-Meditation

Hardening of the heart, like hardening of the arteries, sometimes creeps up on us almost imperceptibly. It did with the Israelites through their much murmuring and complaining. Even after their miraculous exit from four hundred years of captivity, their praise to God was short-lived, and self-centered complaints soon hardened their hearts. A good warning to us, Lord, that our heart attitudes are clearly visible to You.

Moving the Hard Heart

God's Word to Me

Now when they heard this, they were pricked in their heart, and said unto Peter and to the rest of the apostles, Men and brethren, what shall we do?

Acts 2:37, KJV

He who believes in Me, as the Scripture has said, out of his heart will flow rivers of living water.

John 7:38, NKJV

Prayer-Meditation

Lord, so often I have tried fruitlessly to convince and convict others of wrong-doing. This must always be the work of Your Spirit alone. So, Holy Spirit of God, use my mouth to utter the words that will enable You to convict the hearts of men— even as You used Peter—that men may believe and have eternal life.

Winning One Person

God's Word to Me

As the Father has sent Me, I also send you.

John 20:21, NKJV

He said to them, "The harvest is plentiful, but the laborers are few; therefore ask the Lord of the harvest to send out laborers into his harvest."

Luke 10:2, NRSV

Read Matthew 10:5–8.

Prayer-Meditation

Father God, I see that the good news can never win the world for Christ unless every disciple takes his commission as a personal, daily responsibility. It is my feet, my hands, my voice You want to use. Show me to whom You want to send me today, and give me Your words— not mine—for that person.

Friendship with God

God's Word to Me

Now acquaint yourself with Him, and be at peace.

Job 22:21, NKJV

She had a sister named Mary, who sat down at the feet of the Lord and listened to his teaching.

Luke 10:39, TEV

Read Job 42:1–6, 10.

Prayer-Meditation

Father, I am ashamed that I take time for human friendship and neglect Your friendship. I seek now Scripture's answer to the most pertinent question in our world today: what is our God really like?

During this morning hour I would sit at Your feet, Lord Jesus, to acquaint myself with You, and in Your face to see the Father.

Love That Endures

God's Word to Me

[Love] beareth all things, believeth all things, hopeth all things, endureth all things.

1 Corinthians 13:7, KJV

For I have said, "Mercy shall be built up forever; Your faithfulness You shall establish in the very heavens."

Psalm 89:2, NKJV

Prayer-Meditation

The words of this chapter on love convict me, Lord. My love falls far short. But I know that what I cannot do in my own power, You can do through me. So I ask for the unquenchable fire of your love. May it transform everything I do.

Love Your Neighbor

God's Word to Me

The second [commandment] is this, "You shall love your neighbor as yourself."

Mark 12:31, RSV

We love because he first loved us.

1 John 4:19, NRSV

Prayer-Meditation

Thank you, Lord, for helping me see that I cannot love my neighbor properly unless I first love myself. But help me to separate the kind of self-respect that comes from knowing I am a child of the King from the self-love that leads to selfish living and indifference to others.

Seeking Wholeness

God's Word to Me

Behold, thou desirest truth in the inward being; therefore teach me wisdom in my secret heart. . . . Fill me with joy and gladness; let the bones which thou hast broken rejoice.

Psalm 51:6, 8, RSV

If we confess our sins, He is faithful and righteous to forgive us our sins and to cleanse us from all unrighteousness.

1 John 1:9, NASB

Prayer-Meditation

I want a principle within
Of jealous, godly fear,
A sensibility of sin,
A pain to feel it near.

O may the least omission pain
My well instructed soul,
And drive me to the blood
   again
Which makes the wounded
   whole.

Charles Wesley

Marriage Vow

God's Word to Me

Submitting yourselves one to another in the fear of God.

Ephesians 5:21, KJV

He who finds a wife finds what is good and receives favor from the LORD.

Proverbs 18:22, NIV

Prayer-Meditation

Always to seek the highest good for your mate is the sovereign preference of God, in order to build together a life that will bear, in abundance, the fruit of the Holy Spirit.

Lord, I see this as Your plan for every marriage. Help couples make it the divine plan for every home. Show us how our relationships can become closer and stronger each day.

For Parents

God's Word to Me

And, ye fathers, provoke not your children to wrath: but bring them up in the nurture and admonition of the Lord.

Ephesians 6:4, KJV

Train children in the right way, and when old, they will not stray.

Proverbs 22:6, NRSV

Prayer-Meditation

Father God, sometimes we despair about the way "the world" all around us drags our children down. We praise You for telling us how to overcome this: as we parents obediently instruct and nurture our children in Your ways, and are living examples for You every day, then You will fulfill for each child that great promise—"when old, they will not stray."

Poverty

God's Word to Me

Blessed are the poor in spirit, for theirs is the kingdom of heaven.

Matthew 5:3, NKJV

Don't store up treasures here on earth where they can erode away or may be stolen. Store them in heaven where they will never lose their value, and are safe from thieves.

Matthew 6:19–20, TLB

Prayer-Meditation

The world rejects this teaching, saying, "Heaven can wait while I get mine now." Yet Jesus meant this as bedrock teaching for the new believer. The acceptance of our own spiritual and moral poverty is the way to get started with Him.

Thank You, Lord, for showing us that *poverty*, not *possessions*, is the key to Your Kingdom.

Fret Not

God's Word to Me

Do not fret because of evildoers, nor be envious of the workers of iniquity. For they shall soon be cut down like the grass, and whither as the green herb.

Psalm 37:1–2, NKJV

Surely Thou dost set them in slippery places; Thou dost cast them down to destruction.

Psalm 73:18, NASB

Prayer-Meditation

Lord, I need these verses because so many people today seem to get away with their cheating. Thank You for the reminder that all evildoers will be cut down, in Your way and in Your timing. My fretting simply turns my face away from You to those workers of iniquity.

Instead of fretting, I will pray for these people, that they will hate their sin and turn to You.

The Sacrifice of Prayer

God's Word to Me

Now in the morning, having risen a long while before daylight, He went out and departed to a solitary place; and there He prayed.

Mark 1:35, NKJV

My soul yearns for you in the night; in the morning my spirit longs for you. When your judgments come upon the earth, the people of the world learn righteousness.

Isaiah 26:9, NIV

Prayer-Meditation

Lord Jesus, every time I read this Scripture I feel guilty because it is so hard to get up early in the morning. When I do rise early, desiring to have time with You, it takes so long to get my thoughts focused and receptive. Help me, Lord, to overcome wandering thoughts and the desire for sleep—and increase my love for You so much that I'll eagerly want to rise early for communion with You.

Christ's Humanity

God's Word to Me

Let the same mind be in you that was in Christ Jesus, who, though he was in the form of God, did not regard equality with God as something to be exploited, but emptied himself, taking the form of a slave, being born in human likeness.

Philippians 2:5–7, NRSV

Prayer-Meditation

Lord, until I grasp the truth that Your being a true Son of man was but a channel for the Father's power during Your days on earth, I am left only with trying to imitate You. Seeking to follow Your example, to be like You without Your Spirit inside me, would be like a candle trying to imitate the sun.

As You emptied Yourself for the Father's indwelling, I would now empty myself for Your Spirit's indwelling.

Prayer for Children

God's Word to Me

Then little children were brought to Him that He might put His hands on them and pray.

Matthew 19:13, NKJV

But whoever causes one of these little ones who believe in Me to stumble, it is better for him that a heavy millstone be hung around his neck, and that he be drowned in the depth of the sea.

Matthew 18:6, NASB

Prayer-Meditation

My heart was burdened for children this morning, Lord, as I thought of the pollution and false teachings pouring into their minds from television, from motion pictures, and pornographic literature, even through the secularism and godlessness of our schools. I would pray for all children, that parents will guard their minds as well as their bodies from evil.

Protection

God's Word to Me

Put on the whole armor of God. And take . . . the sword of the Spirit, which is the word of God.

Ephesians 6:11, 17, NKJV

None who have faith in God will ever be disgraced for trusting him. But all who harm the innocent shall be defeated.

Psalm 25:3, TLB

Prayer-Meditation

The Word of God, like a sword, protects me from faith-destroyers. But since a good defense needs a strong offense, the Word too can go on the attack, cleanly separating truth from falsehood wherever it is encountered and discerning even unconscious motives and intentions in those around me.

Thank You for reminding me, Lord, to rely on the Word whenever I'm pressed to respond to an accusation.

Protection

God's Word to Me

Put on the whole armor of God. . . . And take the helmet of salvation.

Ephesians 6:11, 17, RSV

Let us draw near to God with a sincere heart in full assurance of faith, having our hearts sprinkled to cleanse us from a guilty conscience and having our bodies washed with pure water.

Hebrews 10:22, NIV

Prayer-Meditation

This word comes through strong and clear, Lord. My salvation is through Jesus Christ, and I can begin each day with a conscience washed clean through repentance. Freedom, joy, and confidence can accompany me wherever I go. A protective helmet for my mind, my salvation wards off the barrage of accusations with which Satan would condemn me.

Protection

God's Word to Me

Put on the whole armor of God. . . . Having put on the breastplate of righteousness. . . .

Ephesians 6:11, 14, RSV

And I for my part have made you today a fortified city, an iron pillar and a bronze wall, against the whole land—against the kings of Judah, its princes, its priests, and the people of the land.

Jeremiah 1:18, NRSV

Prayer-Meditation

Thank You for showing me that righteousness is an attitude of the heart, Lord. I need this breastplate to guard against the cynicism and sensuality of our times. Help me to know how to take moral positions on the issues of our day so that I do not come across as self-righteous.

Joy

God's Word to Me

A merry heart doeth good like a medicine.

Proverbs 17:22, KJV

So the ransomed of the LORD shall return, and come to Zion singing, with everlasting joy on their heads; they shall obtain joy and gladness, and sorrow and sighing shall flee away.

Isaiah 51:11, NKJV

Prayer-Meditation

You have made the day, Lord, and it is beautiful. Help me to bring Your joy to every person I meet.

Waiting

God's Word to Me

But they that wait upon the Lord shall renew their strength; they shall mount up with wings as eagles; they shall run, and not be weary; and they shall walk, and not faint.

Isaiah 40:31, KJV

Therefore I am content with weaknesses, insults, hardships, persecutions, and calamities for the sake of Christ; for whenever I am weak, then I am strong.

2 Corinthians 12:10, NRSV

Prayer-Meditation

Rather than wait, I so often plunge ahead on my own strength, wearing myself out with ambition and strife. God's promise is that if I will wait on His timing, all the ingredients for accomplishment will be there: strength, perspective, vision.

O Lord, I want to redirect my energies and enter into a quiet, peaceful place in relationship to You. And wait.

Love of Righteousness

God's Word to Me

Thou [Jesus] hast loved righteousness, and hated iniquity.

Hebrews 1:9, KJV

To those who sold doves he said, "Get these out of here! How dare you turn my Father's house into a market!"

John 2:16, NIV

Prayer-Meditation

Read for yourselves in the Gospels Jesus' references to the world and you will be persuaded that the stench of this world's sin was ever in His nostrils. . . . For He felt Himself standing in a garden in which life's lovely things were becoming rank and decomposing. It was true then, as now, that lilies that fester are worse than weeds.

Peter Marshall

Lord, I give You permission to change my tastes, my desire-world, so that I too will love righteousness and hate life's spoilage.

Love of Truth

God's Word to Me

Speaking the truth in love, we are to grow up in every way into him who is the head, into Christ.

Ephesians 4:15, RSV

Now, am I trying to win the favor of men, or of God? Do I seek to be a man-pleaser? If I were still seeking popularity with men, I should not be a bondservant of Christ, the Messiah.

Galatians 1:10, AMP

Prayer-Meditation

Father, cleanse me from twisted thinking and deceptive ways so that I will come to love the truth and reflect it in my thoughts, in my actions, and in my words. Give me the courage to speak the truth, the selflessness to relinquish my role as a people-pleaser. Help me to learn to speak truth *only* in love.

Love of Honesty

God's Word to Me

Therefore seeing we have this ministry . . . we faint not; but have renounced the hidden things of dishonesty.

2 Corinthians 4:1–2, KJV

But those who do what is true come to the light, so that it may be clearly seen that their deeds have been done in God.

John 3:21, NRSV

Prayer-Meditation

Lord, as Your light of understanding penetrates my unconscious, I am discovering how much "acceptance" of dishonesty has crept on me unawares. I have not always been vigilant against deception; in fact, I have sometimes condoned it in others when I saw my own desires mirrored in them.

Thank You, Lord, for making it clear that it is only as I stand firmly for open honesty in my personal life that I shall be free to confront dishonesty wherever I find it.

The Servant Role

God's Word to Me

The disciple is not above his master, nor the servant above his lord.

Matthew 10:24, KJV

Though I am free and belong to no man, I make myself a slave to everyone, to win as many as possible.

1 Corinthians 9:19, NIV

Prayer-Meditation

To be a "servant" is hardly the goal of most people in our modern society. Yet today's Christians will generally describe themselves as such in reference to Jesus. Does that imply that we truly are ready to be servants to the people around us? Jesus was. Are we prepared for criticism when we strive to do God's will? Jesus was. Are we willing to be a friend without thought of reciprocation, or even when this effort is turned against us? Jesus was.

Lord Jesus, You and Your presence are the reward of life to me. Let my service to others be done graciously and lovingly as unto You, Master.

False Prophets

God's Word to Me

[The Israelites are] a rebellious people . . . who say to the seers, "Do not see," and to the prophets, "Do not prophesy to us right things; speak to us smooth things, prophesy deceits."

Isaiah 30:9–10, NKJV

Read Galatians 1:8.

Prayer-Meditation

Father, I find inside myself the same soil out of which comes rebellion, even being "stiff-necked," preferring to heed my own counsel rather than Your wisdom.

And all around me I hear false prophets promising material prosperity and problem-free lives in return for a shallow commitment to You.

O Father, give me an aversion to smooth talk and deceits; instead give me a thirst for the pure Gospel and Your uncompromising truth.

Praising Others

God's Word to Me

Submit yourselves for the Lord's sake to every authority instituted among men . . . [and] commend those who do right.

1 Peter 2:13–14, NIV

"Well done, you good and faithful servant!" said his master. "You have been faithful in managing small amounts, so I will put you in charge of large amounts. Come on in and share my happiness!"

Matthew 25:21, TEV

Prayer-Meditation

Father, never before had I known that it is Your directive that we praise them that do right. Yet I find numerous Scriptures in which Jesus gave praise to men who performed acts of kindness, prudence, and obedience (Matthew 20:1–16; 25:14–23). And Paul did not neglect to praise those who were faithful and obedient to his teachings (1 Corinthians 11:1–2; Philippians 4:1). Thank You, Lord, for pointing me toward honest praise when I see that it is due.

My Prayer Requests

God's Answers

July

Witnessing

God's Word to Me

You shall receive power when the Holy Spirit has come upon you.

Acts 1:8, RSV

For I am not ashamed of the gospel, for it is the power of God for salvation to everyone who believes, to the Jew first and also to the Greek.

Romans 1:16, NASB

Prayer-Meditation

Since I have no power of my own, I must rely on Your power, Lord Jesus, in order to be Your witnessing disciple. Prepare me for service, purge me of doubt, cleanse me of all impurity, and saturate me with Your Spirit.

Abiding in the Light

God's Word to Me

I have come as a light into the world, that whoever believes in Me should not abide in darkness.

John 12:46, NKJV

But if we walk in the light, as he is in the light, we have fellowship with one another, and the blood of Jesus, his Son, purifies us from all sin.

1 John 1:7, NIV

Prayer-Meditation

Our Heavenly Father, we thank Thee that we live in a world where light is in control and where darkness is but the absence of light. Help us to keep our eyes upon the sunshine and not upon the shadows, upon the reality of Thy Love and not upon the counterfeits of the Wilderness.

Glenn Clark

Freedom from Tyranny

God's Word to Me

But they have rejected me [Jehovah] from being king over them.

1 Samuel 8:7, RSV

Let every soul be subject to the governing authorities. For there is no authority except from God, and the authorities that exist are appointed by God.

Romans 13:1, NKJV

Prayer-Meditation

Father, the Scripture this morning tells me that the principle of man's absolute authority, whether over encapsuled community-sects or over nations, is neither Your will nor Your way. I see that democracy governed by assemblies of free men could have sprung *only* out of Your teachings.

Father, help us to cherish our freedom in You and the freedom remaining in this nation as a prized gift directly from Your hands. Help us to struggle to maintain it, to vote for it, work for it, fight for it. Father, how grateful we are for our freedom.

Repentance for Our Nation

God's Word to Me

If My people who are called by My name will humble themselves, and pray and seek My face, and turn from their wicked ways, then I will hear from heaven, and will forgive their sin and heal their land.

2 Chronicles 7:14, NKJV

Read Psalm 58:1–2.

Prayer-Meditation

Lord, my heart is grieved for our nation. I am deeply sorry for the lack of integrity in relationships—relationships between the people of this nation and You, and even relationships between individuals. Father, I earnestly repent of our many sins, lest some forget, or in their ignorant rebellion, fail to do so. I pray today that the hearts of Your believers in America will be convicted in order that a healing of this land might begin. And please show my family and me our part in this healing.

Prayer for Nations

God's Word to Me

He shall call upon Me, and I will answer him; I will be with him in trouble; I will deliver him and honor him. With long life I will satisfy him, and show him My salvation.

Psalm 91:15–16, NKJV

Read Genesis 12:1–3; 26:1–5.

Prayer-Meditation

Father, it seems that You mean this for nations as well as for individuals. Abraham and Jacob, for instance, represented nations, and yet You instructed them to pray in this fashion. And You admonish us to pray for those in authority over us. May Your Holy Spirit so move in the hearts and wills of world leaders that they will seek Your counsel and depend upon Your Word to guide them in making decisions.

False Peace

God's Word to Me

. . . The prophets of Israel which prophesy concerning Jerusalem, and which see visions of peace for her, and there is no peace, saith the Lord God.

Ezekiel 13:16, KJV

Read Ezekiel 3:1–23.

Prayer-Meditation

The vision God gave to Ezekiel told of the coming chastisement of Israel. Courageously, this prophet reported God's message as it was, that false prophets were deceiving the people.

Father, I see that we human beings are the same today as in Old Testament times. When Your message is given in honeyed words of reward for us, we listen gladly; otherwise, we want to turn away.

Give us the courage to face truth: that You are holy but also righteous; merciful but also just; that disobedience always results in separation from You.

Obedience

God's Word to Me

At the commandment of the Lord they rested in the tents, and at the commandment of the Lord they journeyed: they kept the charge of the Lord, at the commandment of the Lord by the hand of Moses.

Numbers 9:23, KJV

Make me to know your ways, O LORD; teach me your paths. Lead me in your truth, and teach me, for you are the God of my salvation; for you I wait all day long.

Psalm 25:4–5, NRSV

Prayer-Meditation

When I read how You guided Moses and the Israelites across the desert by a cloud (Numbers 9:15–23), I can see, Lord, that obeying You is the key to a life of fulfillment. I commit my life to Your care. I seek Your daily instructions. I pledge my obedience to Your commands. My desire is to be always under Your cloud of protection.

Faith

God's Word to Me

This is the word of the Lord to Zerubbabel, saying, Not by might, nor by power, but by My Spirit, says the Lord of hosts. For who are you, O great mountain [of human obstacles]?

Zechariah 4:6–7, AMP

Let every valley be lifted up, and every mountain and hill be made low; and let the rough ground become a plain, and the rugged terrain a broad valley.

Isaiah 40:4, NASB

Prayer-Meditation

Lord, "might" and "power" seem so tangible and impressive. I confess to my shame that so often I do trust in the ways of the world, thus seeking to work out my own solutions rather than trusting the Lord of Hosts. Thank You that my particular mountain of human obstacles is no match for You.

God's Guidance

God's Word to Me

The meek will he guide in judgment: and the meek will he teach his way.

Psalm 25:9, KJV

Blessed are the meek, for they will inherit the earth.

Matthew 5:5, NRSV

Prayer-Meditation

Since meekness—teachability—is a prerequisite for receiving Your guidance, Lord, show me how to be meek without being a doormat, how to be humble without being self-righteous.

Turning Darkness to Light

God's Word to Me

I will make darkness light before them, and crooked things straight. These things will I do unto them, and not forsake them.

Isaiah 42:16, KJV

But everything exposed by the light becomes visible, for it is light that makes everything visible. This is why it is said: "Wake up, O sleeper, rise from the dead, and Christ will shine on you."

Ephesians 5:13–14, NIV

Prayer-Meditation

I confess it, Lord, there are dark areas in my life I have not wanted to bring into the light. I see now that if I am to receive Your blessings, all must be laid out before You, nothing hidden. When my worldly nature resists being exposed to light, help me overcome this.

A Time to Listen

God's Word to Me

He maketh me to lie down in green pastures: he leadeth me beside the still waters.

Psalm 23:2, KJV

Of Benjamin he said: "The beloved of the LORD shall dwell in safety by Him, who shelters him all the day long; and he shall dwell between His shoulders."

Deuteronomy 33:12, NKJV

Prayer-Meditation

Is it possible, Lord, that upon occasion You must "make" us to lie down in green pastures to get our attention? I confess that when bedridden or incapacitated by sickness, I feel guilty about duties not performed. Help me to use these occasions to seek Your Word for me. Enable me to see each temporarily closed door as Your leading toward the green pastures and the still waters of a listening ear and a receptive heart.

The High Road

God's Word to Me

There is a way that seems right to a man, but its end is the way of death.

Proverbs 16:25, NKJV

LORD, I have so many enemies! Lead me to do your will; make your way plain for me to follow.

Psalm 5:8, TEV

Prayer-Meditation

Father, these Scriptures remind me of the old Scottish ballad, "You take the high road and I'll take the low road, and I'll be in Scotland 'afore ye." Today there are so many who are preaching "short cuts" to heaven. But Your Word clearly reveals that we cannot use a "low" road to reach a "high" place.

Lord, help me discern the true from the false. Teach me how to lead others onto the "high road" so that they will travel to the place You have prepared for them.

Trust

God's Word to Me

. . . Trust in him [the Lord], and he will act.

Psalm 37:5, RSV

For since the world began no one has seen or heard of such a God as ours, who works for those who wait for him!

Isaiah 64:4, TLB

Prayer-Meditation

What an amazing promise! In return for our trust, God in His supernatural way will bring things to pass which we would never have thought of, or dreamed could take place.

We trust Him, commit ourselves to Him, and then go about our daily walk. He is thus freed to move in our lives and answer our prayers.

Fear of the Lord

God's Word to Me

The fear of the Lord prolongs days . . . is a fountain of life.

Proverbs 10:27; 14:27, NKJV

Love has been perfected among us in this: that we may have boldness on the day of judgment, because as he is, so are we in this world.

1 John 4:17, NRSV

Prayer-Meditation

Father, I confess that I tend to bypass Scriptures that say I should fear You. You see, I do fear You and this makes me feel guilty because I know I want to love You. Can I fear You and love You at the same time?

The answer that comes is— yes. If my fear of You is awe, this is a healthy fear. If my fear of You is negative, then I turn to Your Word . . . perfect love casteth out fear (1 John 4:18).

Being Super-Spiritual

God's Word to Me

Beware of the scribes, who desire to go around in long robes, love . . . the best seats in the synagogues . . . and for a pretense make long prayers.

Mark 12:38–40, NKJV

Prayer-Meditation

Lord, in the caustic vehemence of Your words in today's reading, I hear no Jesus meek and mild—rather the wrath of Jehovah thundering from Mount Sinai.

I hear Your abhorrence of spiritual posturing; of constantly taking my spiritual pulse while neglecting the obvious needs of those around me; of counting myself too super-spiritual to relax and enjoy children and laughter and good fellowship.

Thank You for Your realism, Lord: that as long as I am in this body, I shall never grow wings and will do well to remember my creaturehood; that You want my feet planted firmly on Your good earth.

Serving God

God's Word to Me

Well done, good and faithful servant; you have been faithful over a little, I will set you over much; enter into the joy of your master.

Matthew 25:23, RSV

But we have this treasure in jars of clay to show that this all-surpassing power is from God and not from us.

2 Corinthians 4:7, NIV

Prayer-Meditation

Teach me, O Lord, to do little things as though they were great, because of the majesty of Christ who does them in us and who lives our life; and to do the greatest things as though they were little and easy, because of His Omnipotence.

Pascal

Disciplining the Tongue

God's Word to Me

If any one thinks he is religious, and does not bridle his tongue but deceives his heart, this man's religion is vain.

James 1:26, RSV

When there are many words, transgression is unavoidable, But he who restrains his lips is wise.

Proverbs 10:19, NASB

Read James 3:2–18.

Prayer-Meditation

Lord, I see that the discipline of my tongue is one of Your priority disciplines. This day, keep me alert to those inner checks when I should be silent; to the bridle of Your Spirit when I would speak a destructive or divisive word.

Gossip

God's Word to Me

And the tongue is a fire, a world of iniquity . . . full of deadly poison.

James 3:6, 8, NKJV

A gossip betrays a confidence, but a trustworthy man keeps a secret.

Proverbs 11:13, NIV

Prayer-Meditation

Lord, Your Word is teaching me that the wrong use of the tongue can defile not only my body, but also my family and Your Body—the church fellowship—as well. I dare to ask You to make me a catalyst in my church that together we may be alert to this truth, ever working against gossip and toward love and unity and upbuilding.

Vision

God's Word to Me

Where there is no vision, the people perish.

Proverbs 29:18, KJV

Prayer-Meditation

American missionary Mark Buntain had a vision of Jesus walking the streets of Calcutta, leaning down to one after another of the pathetic, disease-ridden, starving persons there who, having no homes, live and die in the street. With that vision before him, young Mark went to Calcutta. His efforts gave substance to the vision in the form of a hospital, a school, vocational opportunities, and greatest of all, *life* where there was death.

Help me, Lord, to catch Your vision for others and abandon myself to be Your hands, Your feet, Your voice in giving substance to that vision.

Prayer for Strength

God's Word to Me

And Jesus looking upon them saith, With men it is impossible, but not with God: for with God all things are possible.

Mark 10:27, KJV

Finally, be strong in the Lord, and in the strength of His might.

Ephesians 6:10, NASB

Prayer-Meditation

I love this promise, Lord, because it helps me see myself as I am. So often situations bewilder or overwhelm me; I almost feel defeated before I begin to think through possible solutions. Then I remember that You have walked this way before me. Alone I am weak, but You have promised me Your strength. With You there is nothing I can't accomplish.

Our Earthly Treasures

God's Word to Me

Your gold and silver are corroded, and their corrosion will be a witness against you. . . . You have heaped up treasure in the last days.

James 5:3, NKJV

Remember him—before the silver cord is severed, or the golden bowl is broken; before the pitcher is shattered at the spring, or the wheel broken at the well, and the dust returns to the ground it came from, and the spirit returns to God who gave it.

Ecclesiastes 12:6–7, NIV

Prayer-Meditation

One thing is certain, Lord, we cannot take our earthly treasures with us at the end of life. How would You have us handle our possessions as we prepare for the last days? What will we need? What should we get rid of? We know not when You will return, Lord Jesus, but our heart's desire is to be ready.

Sonship

God's Word to Me

So through God you are no longer a slave but a son, and if a son then an heir.

Galatians 4:7, RSV

Prayer-Meditation

I praise You, Father, for the freedom of choice to become a son and an heir rather than a slave of Satan's; that as we voluntarily hand over self-will, You give us back the personality that is uniquely ours. Thank You for delivering us from Satan's slavery that seeks to suck out our selfhood and make us into assembly-line puppets.

Out of the fullness of the Godhead, Lord, Your life spills joyously over into my life. You, Lord, are always positive and creative, ever adding or multiplying, while Satan seeks to destroy and spoil by subtracting.

It is Your pleasure that I, as a child of the King, be distinctly myself, united to You, loving and adoring You. Who but You, Lord, could have thought of that!

In His Presence

God's Word to Me

And Jesus answered and said to her, "Martha, Martha, you are worried and troubled about many things. But one thing is needed, and Mary has chosen that good part, which will not be taken away from her."

Luke 10:41–42, NKJV

She [Martha] said to him, "Yes, Lord, I believe that you are the Christ, the Son of God, who is to come into the world."

John 11:27, NKJV

Prayer-Meditation

Master, recently I have neglected talking with You in prayer and sitting at Your feet to listen, giving busyness and preoccupation with the pots and pans of life as my excuse.

I know now that You have been trying to get my attention through a series of minor mishaps as my life always goes awry when I do not look to You.

Forgive me. Help me now, along with Mary, to choose "the good part"—the best dish.

The Quietness of His Presence

God's Word to Me

In returning and rest shall ye be saved; in quietness and in confidence shall be your strength.

Isaiah 30:15, KJV

Now as they said these things, Jesus Himself stood in the midst of them, and said to them, "Peace to you."

Luke 24:36, NKJV

Prayer-Meditation

Drop thy still dews of quiet-
ness
Till all our strivings cease;
Take from our souls the strain
and stress,
And let our ordered lives con-
fess
The beauty of thy peace.

John Greenleaf Whittier

Dependence upon God

God's Word to Me

Apart from Me you can do nothing.

John 15:5, NASB

The Lord is my strength, my song, and my salvation. He is my God, and I will praise him. He is my father's God—I will exalt him.

Exodus 15:2, TLB

Prayer-Meditation

Lord, this seems a drastic statement until I remember that every breath, every heartbeat is dependent on You. Forgive me for times when, in a rebellious or an arrogant spirit, I have tried to make it on my own. Your truth is that the self-deception of such "independence" is an exercise in futility and a waste of my life.

When in a Storm

God's Word to Me

He rebuked the wind and said to the sea, "Hush, be still." And the wind died down and it became perfectly calm.

Mark 4:39, NASB

Read Psalm 107:29–30.

Prayer-Meditation

Commit thou all that grieves
    thee into the faithful hands
Of Him who never leaves thee,
    Who heaven and earth
    commands;
For He, the clouds' Director,
    Whom winds and seas obey,
Will be thy kind Protector and
    will prepare thy way.

Paulus Gerhardt, 1607–76

Handle the storms of our lives, dear Jesus, as surely as You did that tumultuous sea long ago.

Facing Adversity

God's Word to Me

Though He slay me, I will hope in Him.

Job 13:15, NASB

You who fear the LORD, trust in the LORD; He is their help and their shield.

Psalm 115:11, NASB

Prayer-Meditation

O Lord, You know my plight and my total discomfort in adversity. Use it now to purify my praise of You. I glorify You, not just for what You can do for me, but simply because You are good and holy and are supremely worthy of receiving all glory and honor and praise. I accept Your loving presence even in the midst of real trouble and trust Your goodness, no matter the outcome.

Trial by Fire

God's Word to Me

Beloved, think it not strange concerning the fiery trial which is to try you, as though some strange thing happened unto you.

1 Peter 4:12, KJV

Blessed is anyone who endures temptation. Such a one has stood the test and will receive the crown of life that the Lord has promised to those who love him.

James 1:12, NRSV

Prayer-Meditation

Sometimes, Jesus, when I'm hurting, I think I am paying for a past sin. But You were utterly obedient to our Father, and yet You still suffered deeply, but with grace. Grant that I too may suffer my trial graciously—whether it comes through sin or innocence—and that I may rejoice in the learning experience it provides.

Commitment

God's Word to Me

I will delight myself in Your statutes; I will not forget Your Word.

Psalm 119:16, AMP

But as for you, return to your God, hold fast to love and justice, and wait continually for your God.

Hosea 12:6, NRSV

Prayer-Meditation

What joy and peace reign in me when I actively pursue this commitment, which means that each day begins with a special time alone for saturating myself with Scripture. From then on even the hurts are easier to take and the burden of decisions is lighter.

Ministering Angels

God's Word to Me

For He will give His angels charge concerning you, to guard you in all your ways.

Psalm 91:11, NASB

However, when He, the Spirit of truth, has come, he will guide you into all truth; for He will not speak on His own authority, but whatever He hears He will speak; and He will tell you things to come.

John 16:13, NKJV

Prayer-Meditation

This is a staggering statement, Lord—"to guard you in all your ways"! It's wonderful to realize that You have assigned angels, to help me not only in moments of need, but even when that need has arisen out of my rebellion or disobedience to Your guidance. I pray also that Your angels will deter me from going any way contrary to Your perfect will for my life.

Living Sacrifice

God's Word to Me

I beseech you therefore, brethren, by the mercies of God, that you present your bodies a living sacrifice, holy, acceptable to God.

Romans 12:1, NKJV

The sacrifice acceptable to God is a broken spirit; a broken and contrite heart, O God, you will not despise.

Psalm 51:17, NRSV

Prayer-Meditation

I have always winced, Lord, over this request, probably because bodily comforts mean so much to me. Yet if I have surrendered *all* to You, then I can hold nothing back. Forgive my reluctance here.

So take my body, Lord. Mold it and shape it so that it serves You in the best possible way.

My Prayer Requests

_____

_____

_____

_____

_____

_____

_____

_____

_____

God's Answers

_____

_____

_____

_____

_____

_____

_____

_____

_____

August

Ultimate Truth

God's Word to Me

I know that my Redeemer lives.

Job 19:25, RSV

I am He who lives, and was dead, and behold, I am alive for evermore. Amen. And I have the keys of Hades and of Death.

Revelation 1:18, NKJV

Prayer-Meditation

Jesus my Redeemer, lives!
I, too, unto life must waken.

The Moravian Text

O Lord, may this truth about Christ's crucifixion and resurrection erupt out of the smoldering miseries of our despairing lives with such force as to burn all other pitiable realities in its consuming fire. This clarion call to reality makes all else of so little consequence, praise God!

The Caring Shepherd

God's Word to Me

The Lord . . . is longsuffering toward us, not willing that any should perish but that all should come to repentance.

2 Peter 3:9, NKJV

The LORD is my shepherd, I shall not be in want.

Psalm 23:1, NIV

Prayer-Meditation

I hold to this promise, Lord, for those close to me who are indifferent or who reject You completely. I pray for them: that their closed minds will open to You; that their blinded eyes will see how their wrongdoing is shutting out all the joys and gifts that Your love would give them; that Your loving patience will melt their cold hearts.

Spiritual Warfare

God's Word to Me

For we do not wrestle against flesh and blood, but against principalities, against powers, against the rulers of the darkness of this age, against spiritual hosts of wickedness in the heavenly places.

Ephesians 6:12, NKJV

No one will be able to stand up against you all the days of your life. As I was with Moses, so I will be with you; I will never leave you nor forsake you.

Joshua 1:5, NIV

Prayer-Meditation

O Lord, how I need Your whole armor to live as Your follower in this day and age. All the strength and ingenuity of my human strategy is as nothing. Give me discernment, Father, to know the enemy so that I may quickly appropriate Your defense.

Worship

God's Word to Me

God is spirit; and those who worship Him must worship in spirit and truth.

John 4:24, NASB

Praise the LORD, my soul! All my being, praise his holy name!

Psalm 103:1, TEV

Prayer-Meditation

Why do I let cares and worries weigh me down, Lord, and hide Your face from me? I know what I must do to feel Your Spirit inside me again. It begins with praise. It continues with praise. It ends with praise.

Release for the Captive

God's Word to Me

Now behold, an angel of the Lord stood by him, and a light shone in the prison; and he struck Peter on the side and raised him up, saying, "Arise quickly!" And his chains fell off his hands.

Acts 12:7, NKJV

Read Isaiah 42:6–7.

Prayer-Meditation

Long my imprisoned spirit lay,
Fast bound in sin and nature's
   night:
Thine eye diffused a quicken-
   ing ray,
I woke, the dungeon flamed
   with light:
My chains fell off, my heart
   was free,
I rose, went forth, and followed Thee.

Charles Wesley, 1788

Thank You, Lord, for freeing me from the bondage of my worldly behavior.

The Way Out of the Wilderness

God's Word to Me

Behold, the Lord your God has set the land before you; go up, take possession . . . do not fear or be dismayed.

Deuteronomy 1:21, RSV

Yet the promise remains and some get in—but not those who had the first chance, for they disobeyed God and failed to enter.

Hebrews 4:6, TLB

Prayer-Meditation

Your Word makes it clear, Father, that it was nothing but unbelief and disobedience that kept the Israelites wandering in the wilderness for forty years. Therefore, how long I stay in my particular wilderness depends on me.

Thank You, Father, that believing Your promises, trusting You for the next step, relying on Your supply is the way out of the wilderness for me, so that I can enter the particular promised land that You have prepared.

Christian Humanity

God's Word to Me

Great indeed . . . is the mystery of our religion. He [Jesus] was manifested in the flesh.

1 Timothy 3:16, RSV

Prayer-Meditation

May our prayer, O Christ, awaken all Thy human reminiscences. . . .

Peter Marshall

Awesome indeed, O Lord, is the sharp reality of Your tabernacling in human flesh. You grew as all boys grow: helped in the carpenter shop, learned to fashion perfectly curved yokes for the oxen, knew what it was to be tired, to know hunger and thirst, to have aching muscles. You too felt hot tears running down Your cheeks. On the cross the nails being driven in were as agonizing to Your flesh as to any man's.

I praise You for being my Brother-Christ as well as my Lord.

Spiritual Food

God's Word to Me

Then Jesus called His disciples to Him and said, "I have compassion on the multitude, because they have now continued with Me three days and have nothing to eat."

Matthew 15:32, NKJV

And He humbled you and let you be hungry . . . that He might make you understand that man does not live by bread alone, but man lives by everything that proceeds out of the mouth of the LORD.

Deuteronomy 8:3, NASB

Prayer-Meditation

Father, we are a hungry people today. We try to satisfy our appetite with indulgence in food and drink, with constant reading for knowledge, with sexual excesses. But we are still hungry.

Lord, rather than food for my body, I would be as those who fed only upon Your Word for three days and quenched the thirst of their spirits with Your presence.

149

Our Bulwark against Temptation

God's Word to Me

For we do not have a High Priest who cannot sympathize with our weaknesses, but was in all points tempted as we are, yet without sin.

Hebrews 4:15, NKJV

Prayer-Meditation

Temptation is a test by an alien power of an individual's spiritual resources. Does not this explain the temptations Jesus endured? And does it not also explain the temptations as "joint heirs with Christ" in the Kingdom of God? Had we not, through being "born anew," received into ourselves the very Spirit of God, then Satan would have no interest in us at all. He is after that possession God gave us, that is, the indwelling Christ.

Lord, how grateful I am that Your indwelling Spirit is such a bulwark against all the temptations of Satan.

Mind Renewal

God's Word to Me

And do not be conformed to this world, but be transformed by the renewing of your mind.

Romans 12:2, NKJV

A new heart will I give you, and a new spirit will I put within you: and I will take away the stony heart out of your flesh and give you a heart of flesh.

Ezekiel 36:26, AMP

Prayer-Meditation

A powerful challenge to our materialistic world, Lord. We are in all-out spiritual warfare, with Satan pressing us to conform to his world and You offering renewal and regeneration by the Holy Spirit.

With an act of my will, Lord, I surrender my mind to You for transformation. I seek to be in the perfect will of God.

No Other Gods

God's Word to Me

Thou shalt have no other gods before me.

Exodus 20:3, KJV

Dear children, keep away from anything that might take God's place in your hearts. Amen.

1 John 5:21, TLB

Prayer-Meditation

God—Supreme Being, Sovereign, in control of all creation; Jesus—thank You for being Lord of my life; Holy Spirit—at any moment, in any place, with any person: when I may be tempted to allow something or someone to usurp Your position in my life, alert me, that I may not sin. I would bow only to You—Father, Son, and Holy Spirit.

No Graven Image

God's Word to Me

Thou shalt not make unto thee any graven image . . . for I the Lord thy God am a jealous God.

Exodus 20:4–5, KJV

Woe to the one who quarrels with his Maker—an earthenware vessel among the vessels of the earth! Will the clay say to the potter, "What are you doing?" Or the thing you are making say, "He has no hands"?

Isaiah 45:9, NASB

Prayer-Meditation

Lord, I've usually thought this referred to carved objects—material objects. But sometimes *I* have tried to refashion myself and others instead of allowing You to do Your own work, conforming us all to Your image. I know You are jealous of Your position as God in our lives. I take my hands off. Help me, Lord, to give You freedom to make and remake any and all of us as You will.

The Lord's Name

God's Word to Me

Thou shalt not take the name of the Lord thy God in vain.

Exodus 20:7, KJV

"Then you call on the name of your god and I will call on the name of the LORD; the god who answers by fire is indeed God." All the people answered, "Well spoken!"

1 Kings 18:24, NRSV

Prayer-Meditation

Forgive me for all the times I have used Your name irreverently, Lord . . . in thought or spoken word. Forgive me for the times when I have remained quiet while hearing others curse in Your name. Give me wisdom and courage to handle such situations as Jesus would.

Keeping the Sabbath

God's Word to Me

Remember the sabbath day, to keep it holy.

Exodus 20:8, KJV

He said to them, "This is what the LORD commanded: 'Tomorrow is to be a day of rest, a holy Sabbath to the LORD. So bake what you want to bake and boil what you want to boil. Save whatever is left and keep it until morning.'"

Exodus 16:23, NIV

Prayer-Meditation

How I have failed You here! I go to church, Lord, but during the rest of the day I do little to keep away from the blare and noise and confusion of the world. Recognizing that You have made the Sabbath a day of rest for my benefit, I would seek to be re-created in it and to keep it a Holy Day unto You.

Honor Thy Parents

God's Word to Me

Honour thy father and thy mother: that thy days may be long upon the land which the Lord thy God giveth thee.

Exodus 20:12, KJV

These are the commands, decrees and laws the LORD your God directed me to teach you to observe in the land that you are crossing the Jordan to possess, so that you, your children and their children after them may fear the LORD your God as long as you live by keeping all his decrees and commands that I give you, and so that you may enjoy long life.

Deuteronomy 6:1–2, NIV

Prayer-Meditation

Your great promise of a long life attached to this commandment is often missed, Father. I've pondered the connection and conclude it is based on Your divine plan for the family as the central core of a healthy society. I see so much healing taking place when children obey this commandment.

Not to Kill

God's Word to Me

Thou shalt not kill.

Exodus 20:13, KJV

I know that the LORD maintains the cause of the needy, and executes justice for the poor.

Psalm140:12, NRSV

Prayer-Meditation

It is easy to say, "I am not guilty of this sin." Yet I wonder. What about those murderous thoughts? The drunken driver who snuffs out the life of another would say, "I'm not a killer." But he or she is. How did we feel about our soldiers killing the North Vietnamese? Forgive us for our arrogance, Lord, and forgive me for a hardhearted attitude toward a strange land and a strange people.

Adultery

God's Word to Me

Thou shalt not commit adultery.

Exodus 20:14, KJV

For why should you, my son, be exhilarated with an adulteress, and embrace the bosom of a foreigner? For the ways of a man are before the eyes of the LORD, and He watches all his paths.

Proverbs 5:20–21, NASB

Prayer-Meditation

O Lord, the lust of Sodom seems pale in the face of the degeneration of people today. We have all violated this command in either thought or deed and are in need of Your forgiveness. Today, Father, I pray that You will deliver Your children from adulterous relationships and convince them of their real need of You.

Stealing

God's Word to Me

Thou shalt not steal.

Exodus 20:15, KJV

A just weight and balance are the LORD's; all the weights in the bag are his work.

Proverbs 16:11, NKJV

Prayer-Meditation

Lord, we can be so self-righteous and yet so phony about stealing. We do not take money from a man with a gun; we do it through deceit. We do not steal a friend's car; we rob him of his time and honor and peace of mind. We increase our income by lying to employers and the government and call it being smart. Forgive us our hypocrisy, Lord.

False Witness

God's Word to Me

Thou shalt not bear false witness against thy neighbour.

Exodus 20:16, KJV

When words are many, sin is not absent, but he who holds his tongue is wise.

Proverbs 10:19, NIV

Prayer-Meditation

Forgive me, Lord, for the times I've exaggerated a story about other people as a joke, or allowed a misconception to go by unchecked in order to build myself up at others' expense. Sometimes my secret intent has been to hurt someone purposely. Check my mind, stop my tongue whenever this temptation arises, and grant me the grace, if need be, to go back and correct the lies I have spread.

Covetousness

God's Word to Me

Thou shalt not covet thy neighbour's house . . . thy neighbour's wife . . . nor any thing that is thy neighbour's.

Exodus 20:17, KJV

The desire of the righteous ends only in good; the expectation of the wicked in wrath.

Proverbs 11:23, NRSV

Prayer-Meditation

Lord, sometimes I find the focus of my attention is on envying what my neighbors and friends have. Cleanse me of any ardent covetous desire of another's possessions. Heal me of every obsessive desire for anything except to serve You with all my heart.

Light and Darkness

God's Word to Me

And this is the condemnation, that the light has come into the world, and men loved darkness rather than light.

John 3:19, NKJV

Read Isaiah 42:16.

Prayer-Meditation

God nowhere holds a man responsible for having the heredity of sin. But if when I realize Jesus Christ came to deliver me from it, I refuse to let Him do so, from that moment I begin to get the seal of damnation.

Oswald Chambers

Lord Jesus, give me a love of the light, a loathing of the darkness.

Loving the Unlovely

God's Word to Me

If you love those who love you, what credit is that to you? Even "sinners" love those who love them.

Luke 6:32, NIV

Yet He did not neglect to leave some witness of Himself, for He did you good and kindnesses, and gave you rains from heaven and fruitful seasons, satisfying your hearts with nourishment and happiness.

Acts 14:17, AMP

Prayer-Meditation

This verse in Luke convicts me because there are people who have criticized me whom I do not love. In fact, I confess that I try to avoid them.

Thank You, Lord, for showing me that I also tend to make a tight little island of myself, my family, and close friends. Help me to spread my love to those in need, to those who do not attract me, even to those I dislike.

Grievous Words

God's Word to Me

A soft answer turns away wrath, but a harsh word stirs up anger.

Proverbs 15:1, NKJV

In your anger do not sin; when you are on your beds, search your hearts and be silent.

Psalm 4:4, NIV

Prayer-Meditation

I lay on Your altar, Lord, my tendency to speak grievous words when I am tired or upset. Help me to stop and think before I fire away with both barrels. Remind me that I can quench Your Spirit inside me when I do not let You speak through me.

Forgive

God's Word to Me

And whenever you stand praying, forgive, if you have anything against anyone. . . . But if you do not forgive, neither will your Father who is in heaven forgive your transgressions.

Mark 11:25–26, NASB

Be gentle and ready to forgive; never hold grudges. Remember, the Lord forgave you, so you must forgive others.

Colossians 3:13, TLB

Prayer-Meditation

Jesus, it is with shame that I face You and confess how difficult I find this teaching. It is so humiliating to admit that there is someone I do not want to forgive. Yet I dare not gamble with my salvation that You purchased by such forgiveness—at the cost of Your life.

To Love My Neighbor

God's Word to Me

You shall love your neighbor as yourself.

Mark 12:31, RSV

For God has not given us a spirit of timidity, but of power and love and discipline.

2 Timothy 1:7, NASB

Prayer-Meditation

Because You are all love, Father, You will not tolerate any hardness in me toward anyone. Thank You for the little parable You gave me this morning: the air around us is full of electricity, but this power cannot be harnessed to work for us unless it is grounded. Similarly, the universe is full of Your power, Father. But to transform lives and answer prayer, that power needs to be grounded in us through the love of person to person. So, Father, in my will I allow Your love to become the ground wire for power in all my relationships.

The Peacemakers

God's Word to Me

Blessed are the peacemakers, for they shall be called sons of God.

Matthew 5:9, RSV

If it is possible, so far as it depends on you, live peaceably with all.

Romans 12:18, NRSV

Prayer-Meditation

Lord, make me an instrument
   of Your peace.
Where there is hatred, let me
   sow love;
Where there is injury, pardon;
Where there is doubt, faith;
Where there is despair, hope;
Where there is darkness, light;
And where there is sadness,
   joy.

St. Francis of Assisi

Destructive Tongue

God's Word to Me

But He [Jesus] turned and said to Peter, "Get behind Me, Satan! You are an offense to Me, for you are not mindful of the things of God, but the things of men."

Matthew 16:23, NKJV

I appeal to you, brothers, in the name of our Lord Jesus Christ, that all of you agree with one another so that there may be no divisions among you and that you may be perfectly united in mind and thought.

1 Corinthians 1:10, NIV

Prayer-Meditation

It is a revelation to me, Lord, that Satan can speak through Your own disciple, or members of my family, or through me, so that ill-temper or divisiveness or deceit comes out. Open my eyes to this, Lord. Teach me how to handle it. Please set Your guard around me and my family this day.

Opportunity

God's Word to Me

Therefore, as we have opportunity, let us do good to all.

Galatians 6:10, NKJV

They are to do good, to be rich in good works, generous, and ready to share.

1 Timothy 6:18, NRSV

Prayer-Meditation

I always need to remind myself that in the worst situation and with the most unlikely person, there is a hidden opportunity to be Your disciple. When the moment comes, nudge me, Lord, and reveal to me the good word or the good gift to be given.

Spirit-Led Bible Reading

God's Word to Me

It is the Spirit who gives life; the flesh profits nothing. The words that I speak to you are spirit, and they are life.

John 6:63, NKJV

Like newborn babies, crave pure spiritual milk, so that by it you may grow up in your salvation, now that you have tasted that the Lord is good.

1 Peter 2:2–3, NIV

Prayer-Meditation

What a difference Your Holy Spirit has made in the reading of Scripture! When I read the Bible because it was "something I should do," it was of no profit to me. Now Your Spirit makes the words come alive and gives me such insights that I find it an exciting and exhilarating experience, lasting long after I have closed the book.

Inner Beauty

God's Word to Me

Let not yours be the outward adorning with braiding of hair, decoration of gold, and wearing of robes, but let it be the hidden person of the heart with the imperishable jewel of a gentle and quiet spirit, which in God's sight is very precious.

1 Peter 3:3–4, RSV

Prayer-Meditation

By the quality of her character, Monica (Augustine's mother) won her pagan husband to Christ whereby God made her "beautiful to him, reverently lovable, and wonderful" (St. Augustine's *Confessions*).

It is this hidden person of the heart, O Lord, who matters to You. And yet my outer appearance is a reflection of my inner personhood. Let me take stock: is my outer appearance a commendation for Christ?

The Fullness of Joy

God's Word to Me

In Your presence is fullness of joy; at Your right hand are pleasures forevermore.

Psalm 16:11, NKJV

For the kingdom of God is not food and drink but righteousness and peace and joy in the Holy Spirit. The one who thus serves Christ is acceptable to God and has human approval.

Romans 14:17–18, NRSV

Read Isaiah 55:8–13.

Prayer-Meditation

Joy shining out of the believer's eyes is one of the signs that the King is in residence. Similarly, in prayer, joy is a sign of the Father's approval.

I ask Your forgiveness, Lord, that my joylessness is often such a poor advertisement for Your Kingdom. I ask now that Your joy not be an occasional expression, but a permanent resident in me.

My Prayer Requests

God's Answers

September

The Joy of Work

God's Word to Me

And we labor, working with our own hands.

1 Corinthians 4:12, RSV

Then the LORD God took the man and put him in the garden of Eden to tend and keep it.

Genesis 2:15, NKJV

Read Ephesians 6:5–9.

Prayer-Meditation

Father, one of Your blessings has always been the joy of honest toil. You bade Adam, the first man, "Tend the garden." Jesus Himself must have mended the flat roofs of Nazareth and lovingly fixed toys for the village children. And Paul earned his own way by stitching sails and tents.

Father, let me use my work this day as a worthy sacrament offered up to You.

In Everyday Life

God's Word to Me

Whatever your task, work heartily, as serving the Lord and not men.

Colossians 3:23, RSV

Let nothing be done through selfish ambition or conceit, but in lowliness of mind let each esteem others better than himself.

Philippians 2:3, NKJV

Prayer-Meditation

We look for visions from heaven, for earthquakes and thunders of God's power . . . and we never dream that all the time God is in the commonplace things around us. If we will do the duty that lies nearest, we shall see Him.

Oswald Chambers

I saw your beauty, Lord, in the soapsuds-rainbow of my dishwater. I heard Your voice in a child's laugh. I saw You in the courtesy of the driver who motioned me ahead of him in line, and in the compassionate heart of a friend.

The Empty Self

God's Word to Me

Do not love the world or the things in the world. If any one loves the world, love for the Father is not in him.

1 John 2:15, RSV

Let him not trust in emptiness, deceiving himself; for emptiness will be his reward.

Job 15:31, NASB

Read Mark 8:36.

Prayer-Meditation

Lord, what deadness in my spirit when I have sought pleasures for their own sake! Self-gratification and self-indulgence leave me feeling empty, and yet I am tempted to seek what this world offers. In those moments, remove my blinders so I will see these temptations as shoddy substitutes for the inner riches Your way provides. May Your love always be found in me.

Spiritual Treasure

God's Word to Me

Do not lay up for yourselves treasures on earth, where moth and rust destroy and where thieves break in and steal, but lay up for yourselves treasures in heaven.

Matthew 6:19–20, NKJV

I would feed you with the finest of the wheat, and with honey from the rock I would satisfy you.

Psalm 81:16, NRSV

Read Luke 18:18–27.

Prayer-Meditation

Lord, our hearts are hungry, as are the hearts of people everywhere. Save us from thinking, even for a moment, that we can feed our souls on things. Save us from the vain delusion that the piling up of wealth or comforts can satisfy.

Peter Marshall

And thank You, Lord, for showing us that the way to earthly treasure is in discoveries we make spirit-to-Spirit.

Money in Perspective

God's Word to Me

For the love of money is the root of all evil.

1 Timothy 6:10, KJV

Read 1 Samuel 2:8.

Prayer-Meditation

Thank You, Lord, for this reminder. In a world where money dominates nearly every area of our lives—and even most of our Christian organizations—through an act of my will I now separate my real needs involving money from any love I have of money itself. Help me to see money with Your eyes. Show me how You would use it if You were here on earth today. Enable me to put money and wealth in perspective as belonging to You and entrusted to Your children only for a season.

Gossiping Tongues

God's Word to Me

You shall hide them in the secret place of Your presence from the plots of man; You shall keep them secretly in a pavilion from the strife of tongues.

Psalm 31:20, NKJV

He will redeem me unharmed from the battle that I wage, for many are arrayed against me.

Psalm 55:18, NRSV

Prayer-Meditation

Father, I am under a strange kind of assault from misleading stories and twisted facts. I never before realized how Satan can use the gossiping tongues even of fellow Christians to cause strife and divide your fellowships. Today, for this situation, I claim Your great promise of being hidden in Your secret pavilion and protected by Your own presence.

Forgiveness of Sin

God's Word to Me

If we walk in the light, as he is in the light, we have fellowship with one another, and the blood of Jesus his Son cleanses us from all sin.

1 John 1:7, RSV

Read Psalm 51:14.

Prayer-Meditation

O unapproachable Light, how
    can I fold these guilty hands
    before Thee?
How can I pray to thee with
    lips that have spoken false
    and churlish words?
. . . An unruly tongue:
A fretful disposition:
An unwillingness to bear the
    burdens of others:
An undue willingness to let
    others bear my burdens:
. . . Fine words hiding shabby
    thoughts:
A friendly face masking a cold
    heart.

John Baillie

O Lord, have mercy!

Boldness

God's Word to Me

Then Peter said, "Silver and gold I do not have, but what I do have I give you: In the name of Jesus Christ of Nazareth, rise up and walk." And he took him by the right hand and lifted him up, and immediately his feet and ankle bones received strength.

Acts 3:6–7, NKJV

Pray also for me, that whenever I open my mouth, words may be given me so that I will fearlessly make known the mystery of the gospel, for which I am an ambassador in chains. Pray that I may declare it fearlessly, as I should.

Ephesians 6:19–20, NIV

Prayer-Meditation

The sheer exuberance and boldness of Peter and John toward the crippled man convicts me today, Lord. Only Your Spirit inside us would give us the courage to reach out this way to the ill, to the crippled person. I pray for more boldness, Lord, in my Christian walk.

Giving in Secret

God's Word to Me

When you give to the needy, do not let your left hand know what your right hand is doing, so that your giving may be in secret.

Matthew 6:3–4, NIV

Let each one do just as he has purposed in his heart; not grudgingly or under compulsion; for God loves a cheerful giver.

2 Corinthians 9:7, NASB

Prayer-Meditation

There is an exercise of discipline in these verses I need to ponder, Lord, namely that there is a blessing in secret giving. The difficulty here is that most of us like to be appreciated for our gifts. And we want to receive a tax credit for our contributions. Yet there are ways to give anonymously; I pledge to seek them out for I do not want to miss any blessing You have to offer.

Blocks to Answered Prayer

God's Word to Me

But your iniquities have separated you from your God; and your sins have hidden His face from you.

Isaiah 59:2, NKJV

But when you are praying, first forgive anyone you are holding a grudge against, so that your Father in heaven will forgive you your sins too.

Mark 11:25, TLB

Prayer-Meditation

Father, thank You for the lesson here. After waiting a long, long time for a prayer to be answered, I was alerted to search my heart for any sin blocking the answer. I found some resentment still there against two individuals. Now I am determined to root out any darkness in me that could hide Your face and defeat my prayers.

Atonement

God's Word to Me

And I looked, and behold, in the midst of the throne . . . stood a Lamb as though it had been slain.

Revelation 5:6, NKJV

God presented him as a sacrifice of atonement, through faith in his blood.

Romans 3:25a, NIV

Prayer-Meditation

Let earth and heaven agree,
Angels and men be joined,
To celebrate with me
The Saviour of mankind;
To adore the all-atoning Lamb,
And bless the sound of Jesus'
     name.

O for a trumpet voice,
On all the world to call!
To bid their hearts rejoice
In Him who died for all;
For all my Lord was crucified,
For all, for all my Saviour died.

Charles Wesley, 1788

Repentance

God's Word to Me

And God saw their works, that they turned from their evil way; and God revoked His sentence of evil that He had said that He would do to them . . . for He was comforted . . . concerning them.

Jonah 3:10, AMP

Read 2 Chronicles 7:14.

Prayer-Meditation

God so longs to give blessings to His children. But when we are willfully disobedient, justly He corrects us. As He sent Jonah to call the Ninevites to repentance, so He sends His Holy Spirit to warn us. As we repent and turn again to Him, God is merciful to forgive, always generous to restore His blessing upon us.

Lord, let my heart be as grateful and my spirit rejoice as much for the mercy You show toward another, as for Your gracious, overflowing mercy to me.

Commitment

God's Word to Me

Whatever things are true, whatever things are noble, whatever things are just, whatever things are pure, whatever things are lovely, whatever things are of good report, if there is any virtue and if there is anything praiseworthy—meditate on these things.

Philippians 4:8, NKJV

Prayer-Meditation

Lord, my mind is undisciplined and battered with suggestions from many sources to commit myself to worldly things—things that will not bring peace or a closer relationship to You. Help me to commit myself to the "things" You want for me, to Your set of principles, to Your standard of action, that Your own character might be formed in me.

Protection

God's Word to Me

Put on the whole armor of God . . . having girded your loins with truth.

Ephesians 6:11, 14, RSV

And the devil said to Him, "If You are the Son of God, tell this stone to become bread." And Jesus answered him, "It is written, 'Man shall not live on bread alone.'"

Luke 4:3–4, NASB

Prayer-Meditation

Lord, how marvelous to be encircled by Your truth—the only ultimate fortress for freedom in our sin-sick world (John 8:32). Thus equipped, we can stand against Satan, the father of lies. With his deceptions he seeks to weaken our faith in God's love for us and power to help us, and by sowing doubts and fear, make us yet more vulnerable to his attacks.

Thank You for Your promise that when we hurl truth in Satan's face, this forces him to flee.

Giving Correction

God's Word to Me

Fathers, don't scold your children so much that they become discouraged and quit trying.

Colossians 3:21, TLB

He who heeds discipline shows the way to life, but whoever ignores correction leads others astray.

Proverbs 10:17, NIV

Prayer-Meditation

We know how important it is to discipline children, Lord, but we need Your wisdom to know how to correct them in love. Help me not to be permissive at one extreme or a harassing parent at the other.

Courage to Fight Evil

God's Word to Me

I do not pray that thou shouldst take them out of the world, but that thou shouldst keep them from the evil one.

John 17:15, RSV

You have also given me the shield of Your salvation; Your right hand has held me up, Your gentleness has made me great.

Psalm 18:35, NKJV

Prayer-Meditation

In His high-priestly prayer, Jesus did not ask the Father for followers who would seclude themselves from the world, fleeing evil, primarily concerned about their own sanctity or even their Christian growth. Rather Jesus wants to train His followers to go out into the world and take the initiative against evil, armed with His own prayer for their protection against Satan.

Let my spirit, Lord, partake of Your boldness as I go out in the strength of the Father's protection.

Light Overcomes Darkness

God's Word to Me

You are the salt of the earth; but if salt has lost its taste, how can its saltiness be restored? It is no longer good for anything, but is thrown out and trampled under foot. You are the light of the world. A city built on a hill cannot be hid. No one after lighting a lamp puts it under the bushel basket, but on the lampstand, and it gives light to all in the house.

Matthew 5:13–15, NRSV

Prayer-Meditation

Christ's commission to us is not to shut ourselves from the world—rather "to go out *into* all the world." We are to be the salt-preservative in a decaying society, to be light set high on the lampstand for all to see. For darkness must always flee before the light.

Lord, help me to be light in the world, not to draw attention to myself or to my good works, but to put the spotlight on You!

Freedom to Choose

God's Word to Me

What is man that You are mindful of him? . . . For You have made him a little lower than the angels, and You have crowned him with glory and honor.

Psalm 8:4–5, NKJV

Read Deuteronomy 30:19–20a.

Prayer-Meditation

Father, You are reminding me this morning that one major difference exists between man and beasts: the human will—the ability to decide and to choose.

Father, thank You for Your insistence that I come to You voluntarily—or not at all. It awes me to realize that not even the Lord of glory will ever forcibly invade that central citadel of my selfhood—where You planted the decision-making process of my will. This mark of Your greatness alone would make me want to worship You.

Thank You for the reality of such freedom in You.

The Authority of Jesus

God's Word to Me

And they were astonished at his [Jesus'] teaching, for he taught them as one who had authority, and not as the scribes.

Mark 1:22, RSV

Read Mark 10:21.

Prayer-Meditation

Lord Jesus, in Your dealings with me I have felt not only the same "authority" mentioned so often in the Gospels but also the impact of Your compelling, well-nigh irresistible personality. Yet Your attitude toward me, as toward many another, has always been a sharp hands-off: "It's up to you to decide whether or not you obey. I shall not force you or stampede you. *You* decide." So that was why You could stand silently, watching the rich young ruler walk away from You.

Thank You for demonstrating to us so clearly the difference between true authority and the authoritarianism of force.

False Leadership

God's Word to Me

But I tell you, Do not swear at all: either by heaven, for it is God's throne; or by the earth, for it is his footstool; or by Jerusalem, for it is the city of the Great King.

Matthew 5:34–35, NIV

Nor are you to be called "teacher," for you have one Teacher, the Christ.

Matthew 23:10, NIV

Prayer-Meditation

These verses are warning us not to swear allegiance to self-proclaimed prophets, holy men, gurus, and leaders of cults, especially if they demand vows of obedience to them. We know too many horror stories of innocent people corrupted and even destroyed when they let such "leaders" gain control of their lives.

I am grateful, Lord, that I can claim You and You alone as my Master and Lord.

Faith

God's Word to Me

Why standest thou afar off, O Lord? why hidest thou thyself in times of trouble?

Psalm 10:1, KJV

And I will bring the blind by a way that they know not; I will lead them in paths that they have not known. I will make darkness light before them, and uneven places a plain. These things I have determined to do for them, and not leave them forsaken.

Isaiah 42:16, AMP

Prayer-Meditation

Eternal God . . . When the way seems dark before me, give me grace to walk trustingly:
When the distant scene is clouded, let me rejoice that at least the next step is plain. . . .
When insight falters, let me obedience stand firm:
What I lack in faith, let me repay in love. . . .

John Baillie

False Prophets

God's Word to Me

Beware of false prophets, which come to you in sheep's clothing, but inwardly they are ravening wolves.

Matthew 7:15, KJV

But even if we or an angel from heaven should proclaim to you a gospel contrary to what we proclaimed to you, let that one be accursed!

Galatians 1:8, NRSV

Read 1 John 4:1–3.

Prayer-Meditation

I especially hear Your warning for our time, Lord, for false prophets are appearing everywhere, often spouting Scripture, offering quick-and-easy promises. Thank You for giving us the definitive test to apply: Beware of any self-proclaimed prophet who does not confess that Jesus Christ is come in the flesh. And we listen to such a prophet's teaching or follow him with grave danger.

Truth and Error

God's Word to Me

Let both grow together until the harvest. . . . I will say to the reapers, "First gather together the tares and bind them in bundles to burn them."

Matthew 13:30, NKJV

Read Psalm 25:4–5.

Prayer-Meditation

Lord, many of us are troubled about the teaching and witness of certain groups, cults, and communities that call themselves Christian. Your answer, Lord, is another example of Your ways not being our ways: wheat and tares, truth and error, are growing together in these places. The first young shoots look alike; to pull up the tares ruthlessly would damage the wheat too.

We are to await Your timing, the harvest, then the tares (the error or Satan) stand out, easily distinguishable, good only for the fire.

Lord, thank You that You *will* deal with the tares.

Christian Character

God's Word to Me

Therefore you shall be perfect, just as your Father in heaven is perfect.

Matthew 5:48, NKJV

But if we live in the light—just as he is in the light—then we have fellowship with one another, and the blood of Jesus, his Son, purifies us from every sin.

1 John 1:7, TEV

Prayer-Meditation

The expression of Christian character is not good doing, but God-likeness. If the Spirit of God has transformed you within, you will exhibit Divine characteristics in your life, not good human characteristics. God's life in us expresses itself as *God's* life, not as human life trying to be godly . . . and the experience of this works out in the practical details of life. . . .

Oswald Chambers

Persistence in Prayer

God's Word to Me

Now don't be afraid, go on believing.

Luke 8:50, PHILLIPS

Read Luke 11:5–13; 18:7.

Prayer-Meditation

When Jesus promised us, "Knock, and it [the door] shall be opened unto you" (Luke 11:9), He implied that there is a time when the door remains shut. So many of us experience this in prayer. We have prayed with all the faith we can muster about a certain problem, but so far there has been no response from God. It is at this point that persistence on our part must go hand in hand with faith. We must keep pressing forward— "go on believing." Jesus never promised us that the door would be opened at our first tap or in our timing.

Lord, strengthen in me this kind of persistence to give me stalwart faith-muscles.

Mountain-Moving Prayer

God's Word to Me

If you have faith as a mustard seed, you will say to this mountain, "Move from here to there," and it will move; and nothing will be impossible for you.

Matthew 17:20, NKJV

"For nothing will be impossible with God." Then Mary said, "Here am I, the servant of the Lord; let it be with me according to your word."

Luke 1:37–38a, NRSV

Prayer-Meditation

Thank You for demonstrating, Lord, that You do not want us to spiritualize our problems and bow down before mountains of evil; that instead You came to demonstrate the art of mountain-moving. We sense in You, Lord, an exuberant faith and a buoyant humor that says, "So that's your problem. There's nothing here that My Father and I can't handle. Come, let us together blast away the mountain."

Overcoming Discouragement

God's Word to Me

So up with your listless hands!
Strengthen your weak knees!
And make straight paths for
your feet.

Hebrews 12:12–13, MOFFATT

Read Psalm 28:2.

Prayer-Meditation

Discouragement and dejec-
tion are signs of sickness of
spirit (usually not a major illness—just the spiritual sniffles).
Sometimes Satan trips us into
this sad state by feeding our
wounded self-love. Or we have
a demanding spirit, conducting
ourselves before God like a sulk-
ing child demanding what he
wants *now*.

Lord, I see it! In my will I
choose to give up the luxury of
discouragement, and I do now
deliberately raise my listless
hands to You in praise. Thank
You, Lord.

Caring for Others

God's Word to Me

And be kind to one another, ten-
derhearted, forgiving one another, just as God in Christ also
forgave you.

Ephesians 4:32, NKJV

Then this message from the
Lord came to Zechariah. "Tell
them to be honest and fair—and
not to take bribes—and to be
merciful and kind to everyone."

Zechariah 7:8–9, TLB

Prayer-Meditation

Lord, I confess that my heart
is not always tender and kind
toward those who do not love or
please me. Since a melting
process is needed inside my
heart, please give me as a gift,
the tenderness, the kindness,
the generosity of Spirit You show
to all of us.

Ministering Angels

God's Word to Me

And He was there in the wilderness forty days, tempted by Satan, and was with the wild beasts; and the angels ministered to Him.

Mark 1:13, NKJV

Are they not all ministering spirits sent forth to minister for those who will inherit salvation?

Hebrews 1:14, NKJV

Prayer-Meditation

I'm grateful, Father, for the reminder that not only did Your angels protect Jesus in the wilderness, but that You have given the angels charge over us to keep us from falling (Psalm 91:11–12). Thank You for such loving care.

My Secret Place

God's Word to Me

He who dwells in the secret place of the Most High shall abide under the shadow of the Almighty. I will say of the Lord, "He is my refuge and my fortress; my God, in Him I will trust."

Psalm 91:1–2, NKJV

For you have died and your life is hidden with Christ in God.

Colossians 3:3, NASB

Prayer-Meditation

These words roll over me like deep water, bringing such refreshment. Even in the midst of a busy office with ringing telephones, sharp voices, tensions, and frustrations of people at work, I thank You, Father, that You offer me a "secret place" to enter and abide with You.

My Prayer Requests

_____

_____

_____

_____

_____

_____

_____

_____

_____

God's Answers

_____

_____

_____

_____

_____

_____

_____

_____

_____

October

Fearing God

God's Word to Me

But the Lord of hosts, him you shall regard as holy; let him be your fear, and let him be your dread.

Isaiah 8:13, RSV

He said, "Do not lay your hand on the boy or do anything to him; for now I know that you fear God, since you have not withheld your son, your only son, from me."

Genesis 22:12, NRSV

Prayer-Meditation

The Bible is full of reminders that we are to have a "fear of God." This awe and reverence for our Maker leads us to obedience not only because we recognize His almighty power, but also His amazing love for us.

O Lord, I bow before You in awe, honoring You as God and presenting to You the gift of an obedient heart.

Loving God

God's Word to Me

"Because he loves me," says the LORD, "I will rescue him; I will protect him, for he acknowledges my name."

Psalm 91:14, NIV

How great is the love the Father has lavished on us, that we should be called children of God! And that is what we are! The reason the world does not know us is that it did not know him.

1 John 3:1, NIV

Prayer-Meditation

What a promise, Lord, that it is not because of any of our great works but solely because we love You that You will protect us. It would seem to be a reward out of all proportion, but then we remember, "For God so loved the world that He *gave!*" Extravagantly! Beyond human comprehension!

Knowing God

God's Word to Me

Who do men say that I, the Son of Man, am? . . . But who do you say that I am?

Matthew 16:13, 15, NKJV

That I may know Him and the power of his resurrection, and the fellowship of His sufferings, being conformed to His death, if, by any means, I may attain to the resurrection from the dead.

Philippians 3:10–11, NKJV

Prayer-Meditation

Lord, all around me today I hear Your rapier-like question being asked: "Who do *you* say that I am?" For there is much fascination with other religions, other prophets, gurus, exotic rituals. I am hearing, "What difference will it make to me and my problems to believe that Jesus Christ is the Son of God?" The difference is like life and death. Give me the gift of Your wisdom to communicate Your answer to those around me so that they will hear and believe.

Heart Examination

God's Word to Me

Search me, O God, and know my heart: try me, and know my thoughts: And see if there be any wicked way in me.

Psalm 139:23–24, KJV

This third I will bring into the fire; I will refine them like silver and test them like gold. They will call on my name and I will answer them; I will say, "They are my people," and they will say, "The LORD is our God."

Zechariah 13:9, NIV

Prayer-Meditation

Lord, Thou canst see the hidden things in every heart. If our intentions are good, help us to make them live in good deeds. If what we intend or desire makes us uncomfortable in Thy presence, take it from us and give us the spirit we ought to have that we may do what we ought to do.

Peter Marshall

Idolatry

God's Word to Me

So the Lord alone did lead him, and there was no strange god with him.

Deuteronomy 32:12, KJV

What's the use of an idol? It is only something that a man has made, and it tells you nothing but lies. What good does it do for its maker to trust it—a god that can't even talk.

Habakkuk 2:18, TEV

Prayer-Meditation

Lord, I know how easy it is for other gods to become so important that they block me from following You. Such gods as: money, clothes, jewelry, home, car, work, the idolatry of any relationship, enslavement to a habit, pride in position. Since I want You alone to lead me, please correct me if I become distracted.

The Living Word

God's Word to Me

You search the Scriptures, for in them you think you have eternal life; and these are they which testify of Me. But you are not willing to come to Me that you may have life.

John 5:39–40, NKJV

Having been born again, not of corruptible seed but incorruptible, through the word of God which lives and abides forever.

1 Peter 1:23, NKJV

Read John 1:1, 14.

Prayer-Meditation

Lord, You are ever the Realist. You would alert me in the above verses that being a fine Bible student is important all right, but that I must always continue on from the written Word to the living Word. This day I bow to You as the "Word Incarnate," eager to receive from You the living water.

Sharing the Good News

God's Word to Me

How beautiful are the feet of them that preach the gospel of peace, and bring glad tidings of good things!

Romans 10:15, KJV

How beautiful upon the mountains are the feet of the messenger who announces peace, who brings good news, who announces salvation, who says to Zion, "Your God reigns."

Isaiah 52:7, NRSV

Prayer-Meditation

Thank You, Lord, for this beautiful commission to service. The apostles continually rejoiced in telling others the good news of salvation through Jesus Christ. Help me to carry this message today with the same joyous Spirit, a clean heart, a straight tongue, and a warm smile.

Christ's Humanity

God's Word to Me

I assure you . . . the Son is able to do nothing from Himself—of His own accord; but He is able to do only what He sees the Father doing.

John 5:19, AMP

I assure you, most solemnly I tell you, if any one steadfastly believes in Me, he will himself be able to do the things that I do; and he will do even greater things than these, because I go to the Father.

John 14:12, AMP

Prayer-Meditation

Do we really believe Jesus? That of Himself, He was as helpless as we are to perform miracles? That His wonder-working power came only as the result of the Father in Him?

Lord, I see that unless I do believe You here, a promise like John 14:12 makes no sense. As the Father in You did the works, so You intend for the Holy Spirit in me to do the works. What a glorious plan!

Sharing the Good News

God's Word to Me

Now therefore go, and I will be with your mouth and teach you what you shall speak.

Exodus 4:12, RSV

But the Lord said, "Go and do what I say. For Paul is my chosen instrument to take my message to the nations and before kings, as well as to the people of Israel."

Acts 9:15, TLB

Prayer-Meditation

Lord, this is the reassurance to which I will hold in the days ahead. With You in me I have no fear of people, of places, or of the future. Help me to remember this promise and to claim it for particular situations.

Gathering the Harvest

God's Word to Me

Pray the Lord of the harvest to send out laborers into His harvest.

Luke 10:2, NKJV

To the weak I became as weak, that I might win the weak. I have become all things to all men, that I might by all means save some. Now this I do for the gospel's sake, that I may be partaker of it with you.

1 Corinthians 9:22–23, NKJV

Prayer-Meditation

One of the few specific things Jesus asked us to pray for was for people who would be His representatives to reach and win unbelievers—for laborers to help gather in the harvest. Jesus needs a great host of us to be His hands, His feet, His voice, the channels of His Spirit for teaching, counseling, ministering, preaching, healing the sick.

Lord, I see that the harvest can never be gathered in unless each one of us takes our commission seriously as a personal, daily responsibility.

Healing Power

God's Word to Me

But if the Spirit of Him who raised Jesus from the dead dwells in you, He who raised Christ from the dead will also give life to your mortal bodies through His Spirit who dwells in you.

Romans 8:11, NKJV

Jesus said to them again, "Peace be with you. As the Father has sent me, so I send you." When he had said this, he breathed on them and said to them, "Receive the Holy Spirit."

John 20:21–22, NRSV

Prayer-Meditation

O gracious Holy Spirit, I invite You to enter into me. Invade every cell of my mortal body, even as Your power invaded the tomb on Resurrection morning to revive the physical body of Jesus. I accept the fact that it is Your Spirit that gives life, else the flesh profits nothing. I praise You for this new understanding of Your healing power.

The Healing Word

God's Word to Me

He sent forth his word, and healed them, and delivered them from destruction.

Psalm 107:20, RSV

When evening came they brought to Him many who were under the power of demons, and he drove out the spirits with a word, and restored to health all who were sick.

Matthew 8:16, AMP

Read Luke 7:1–10.

Prayer-Meditation

Father, how wonderful it is that You created planets and galaxies and the incredible human body by sending forth Your Word! My prayer is that as You healed the sick and the broken ones when You were here in the flesh, You will send forth Your special Word of healing and restoration now for ————————.

Self-Deception

God's Word to Me

The tongue is a little member and boasts great things. See how great a forest a little fire kindles!

James 3:5, NKJV

So then, as the scripture says, "Whoever wants to boast must boast of what the Lord has done."

1 Corinthians 1:31, TEV

Prayer-Meditation

I told myself: this doesn't apply to me, because I am not given to boasting. But then through prayer You showed me how often I use my tongue with people for quiet self-promotion. Help me to boast only about You and Your greatness and faithfulness.

Two Who Agree

God's Word to Me

Again, I tell you that if two of you on earth agree about anything you ask for, it will be done for you by my Father in heaven. For where two or three come together in my name, there am I with them.

Matthew 18:19–20, NIV

Read 1 Corinthians 1:10.

Prayer-Meditation

During the last week, Lord, You have been showing us another facet of the power of agreement among Christians. When two or more of us "agree" lovingly, positively, clearly within the framework of Your will, then You have promised always to be present. And that the prayer will be answered (Matthew 18:19).

But when such a group of believers "agrees" negatively—usually criticizing or gossiping or judging self-righteously—then instantly Your presence is withdrawn. This then means that the door is opened to Satan and his designs.

Thoughtless Words

God's Word to Me

I tell you, on the day of judgment men will render account for every careless word they utter.

Matthew 12:36, RSV

May the LORD cut off all flattering lips, the tongue that makes great boasts, those who say, "With our tongues we will prevail; our lips are our own—who is our master?"

Psalm 12:3–4, NRSV

Prayer-Meditation

I am beginning to see, Lord, that the gift of speech is precious in Your sight and that You hold me accountable for it. Keep me today from gossip, from thoughtless words that hurt another. Thank You for the gift of speech. May I use it to uplift and edify others.

Christ's Humanity

God's Word to Me

He entered a certain village; and a woman named Martha welcomed Him into her home.

Luke 10:38, NASB

Prayer-Meditation

God gave all men all earth to love,
But since our hearts are small,
Ordained for each one spot should prove
Beloved over all.

Rudyard Kipling

Like all of us, the human Jesus had a favorite spot—the home of Mary, Martha, and Lazarus in the village of Bethany, only a hilly mile or two from Jerusalem.

Bethany marked the start of His triumphant entry into Jerusalem; it was from there that He ascended into heaven.

Knowing of His spot "beloved over all" draws us very close to Him. Our hearts understand!

189

Cleansing of the Heart

God's Word to Me

Watch over your heart with all diligence, for from it flow the springs of life. Put away from you a deceitful mouth.

Proverbs 4:23–24, NASB

For out of the heart come evil thoughts, murder, adultery, sexual immorality, theft, false testimony, slander.

Matthew 15:19, NIV

Prayer-Meditation

I see, Lord, that You hold me responsible for a decision of will to watch over my heart with all diligence. This morning I make that decision even as I ask for Your strength to implement it. Free my mind from any over-emphasis on fleshly desires; keep me free from cynicism, from impure thoughts or fantasies. Help me to bridle my tongue the next time I am tempted to be critical or devious or try to impress another.

Never Lose Hope

God's Word to Me

Why are you cast down, O my soul, and why are you disquieted within me? Hope in God; for I shall again praise him, my help and my God.

Psalm 43:5, RSV

Satisfy us in the morning with your steadfast love, so that we may rejoice and be glad all our days.

Psalm 90:14, NRSV

Prayer-Meditation

Let us not lose the savour of past mercies and past pleasures; but like the voice of a bird singing in the rain, let grateful memory survive in the hour of darkness.

Robert Louis Stevenson

Hospitality

God's Word to Me

Let brotherly love continue. Be not forgetful to entertain strangers: for thereby some have entertained angels unawares.

Hebrews 13:1–2, KJV

Beloved, you are acting faithfully in whatever you accomplish for the brethren, and especially when they are strangers.

3 John 5, NASB

Prayer-Meditation

With evil so rampant today, Lord, I sometimes tend to avoid contact with strangers. Since I want to be generous and open, give me the gift of discernment so that I will be hospitable to those You send my way.

The Power of His Name

God's Word to Me

Therefore God has highly exalted him [Jesus] and bestowed on him the name which is above every name.

Philippians 2:9, RSV

And then I heard everyone in heaven and earth, and from the dead beneath the earth and in the sea, exclaiming, "The blessing and the honor and the glory and the power belong to the one sitting on the throne, and to the Lamb forever and ever."

Revelation 5:13, TLB

Prayer-Meditation

I can never hear enough, Lord, about the incredible power in the name of Jesus—how all in heaven bow at this name, and all of hell must shrink back when it is spoken. I would scale the heights of adoration in singing or speaking of Jesus. And in every need, every emergency, may I never forget to call out the name of Jesus.

Praise

God's Word to Me

And he hath put a new song in my mouth, even praise unto our God: many shall see it, and fear, and shall trust in the Lord.

Psalm 40:3, KJV

For I will [fully] satisfy the weary soul, and I will replenish every languishing and sorrowful person.

Jeremiah 31:25, AMP

Prayer-Meditation

It is the wind of Your Spirit, Lord, that brings refreshment and renewal. I ask now for a new song in my mouth, so that I can praise You for all the ways You have blessed my life.

The Prayer That Upholds

God's Word to Me

It is before his own Master that he stands or falls. And he shall stand and be upheld, for the Master—the Lord—is mighty to support him and make him stand.

Romans 14:4, AMP

Our steps are made firm by the LORD, when he delights in our way; though we stumble, we shall not fall headlong for the LORD holds us by the hand.

Psalm 37:23–24, NRSV

Prayer-Meditation

Lord, I need this strong word of encouragement this morning. You know how troubled I have been about _____. It is hard to stand by and watch one I care about so deeply going down such a destructive path.

I sing praises now that You are undergirding _____. As You support _____, this person cannot and will not fail.

Let God Do It

God's Word to Me

And Moses said . . . "Fear not, stand firm, and see the salvation of the Lord, which he will work for you today."

Exodus 14:13, RSV

Lift up your eyes to the heavens, look at the earth beneath; the heavens will vanish like smoke, the earth will wear out like a garment and its inhabitants die like flies. But my salvation will last forever, my righteousness will never fail.

Isaiah 51:6, NIV

Prayer-Meditation

O Spirit of God, I look to You to do in me what I cannot do for myself. As this day presents new demands, I will live in You, and You will do through me what is required. I must not try, but trust; must not struggle, but rest. Then will Your salvation be seen.

Relinquishment

God's Word to Me

But I will give your life to you as a prize in all places, wherever you go.

Jeremiah 45:5, NKJV

For whoever desires to save his life will lose it, and whoever loses his life for My sake will find it.

Matthew 16:25, NKJV

Prayer-Meditation

Father, enable me to abandon my life to You as Jesus abandoned His life to You when He suffered on the cross. For only then can I see this beautiful Scripture become real. As Your life, flowing through the Holy Spirit, becomes my life, I will attract to me all the good of Your perfect will—whatever You want me to experience at any time, in any place.

Rejoice

God's Word to Me

Be glad, O sons of Zion, and rejoice in the Lord, your God.

Joel 2:23, RSV

May you always be joyful in your union with the Lord. I say it again: rejoice!

Philippians 4:4, TEV

Prayer-Meditation

Scripture tells us over and over to rejoice. It doesn't tell us to act joyfully just when we have been blessed or are successful or have good health. We are to rejoice in the Lord always, regardless of how bad we feel or how poorly life is treating us. A hard teaching, Lord, but I know it's the key to working through those down periods.

The Gift of Grace

God's Word to Me

And the serpent said to the woman, "You will not surely die. For God knows that in the day you eat of it your eyes will be opened, and you will be like God, knowing good and evil."

Genesis 3:4–5, NKJV

Read Romans 5:15.

Prayer-Meditation

Father, I see that the stain of sin inherited from our ancestor Adam is not so much immorality and dishonesty as it is claiming my right to myself, to do what I please, to be my own god. It was to put *that* away that You died on the cross for me.

Therefore, I have no "rights" because to You alone I owe life itself, every breath I draw, the ability to think, to move, to love, every talent I possess.

Your grace and goodness to all of us are incredible! Lord, I bow before You in adoration.

Our Unchanging God

God's Word to Me

While the earth remaineth, seedtime and harvest, and cold and heat, and summer and winter, and day and night shall not cease.

Genesis 8:22, KJV

In the day of my trouble I will call to you, for you will answer me.

Psalm 86:7, NIV

Prayer-Meditation

The revolving seasons, the inevitability of day and night, eloquently speak to me, Father, of our God who changest not....

God of our life, through all the
circling years, we trust in
Thee.
In all the past, through all our
hopes and fears, Thy hand
we see.
With each new day, when
morning lifts the veil,
We own Thy mercies, Lord,
which never fail.

Hugh T. Kerr

The Reality of His Presence

God's Word to Me

And lo, I am with you all the days,—perpetually, uniformly and on every occasion.

Matthew 28:20, AMP

You provide delicious food for me in the presence of my enemies. You have welcomed me as your guest; blessings overflow!

Psalm 23:5, TLB

Prayer-Meditation

You, Lord, are more than an idea or an influence, more than a great teacher or a guiding power: You are an alive, real Person—my Companion and Friend. And there is a constancy about Your presence that does not depend on my feelings or on what I am doing. Thank You for being so real and ever present.

Obedience

God's Word to Me

But Peter and the apostles [when accused by the High Priest] answered, "We must obey God rather than men."

Acts 5:29, RSV

So we may boldly say: "The Lord is my helper; I will not fear. What can man do to me?"

Hebrews 13:6, NKJV

Prayer-Meditation

Imagine the fearless confidence of these apostles given them by the Holy Spirit as they stood before the council in Jerusalem and took their stand for Jesus Christ!

When the moment of testing comes for me, Lord, I too want the infusion of the Spirit's power for this kind of obedience.

Help in Trouble

God's Word to Me

God is our refuge and strength, a very present help in trouble.

Psalm 46:1, KJV

Then the LORD turned to him and said, "Go in this might of yours and deliver Israel from the hand of Midian; I hereby commission you."

Judges 6:14, NRSV

Prayer-Meditation

Lord, what comfort this verse in Psalm 46 has brought to me—twelve words to cling to when things go wrong. You are indeed my "hiding place" in times of trouble. And when I am totally weak, I feel Your strength moving me into the action. All I have to do is call Your name and there You are.

Jesus' Prayer for Us

God's Word to Me

Holy Father, keep through Your name those whom You have given Me, that they may be one as We are.

John 17:11, NKJV

Do not conform any longer to the pattern of this world, but be transformed by the renewing of your mind. Then you will be able to test and approve what God's will is—his good, pleasing and perfect will.

Romans 12:2, NIV

Prayer-Meditation

Jesus reaches here to the ultimate of Your sovereignty, Lord, to plead our cause. He knows that Satan attacks those who belong to You, not those in his world. Jesus also knows that we need His intercession for our protection and Christian growth.

Thank You for the reassurance that as we are kept in the holiness of God, we will be transformed into Your likeness—"that they may be one, as We are."

197

My Prayer Requests

_____
_____
_____
_____
_____
_____
_____
_____
_____
_____

God's Answers

_____
_____
_____
_____
_____
_____
_____
_____
_____
_____
_____

November

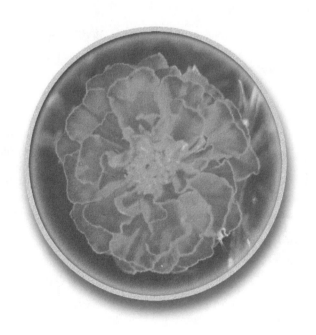

God Is with You

God's Word to Me

Be strong and of good courage; do not be afraid, nor be dismayed, for the Lord your God is with you wherever you go.

Joshua 1:9, NKJV

For I was ashamed to request of the king a band of soldiers and horsemen to protect us against the enemy along the way; because we had told the king, The hand of our God is upon all them for good who seek Him, but His power and His wrath are against all those who forsake Him.

Ezra 8:22, AMP

Prayer-Meditation

We need this promise today, Lord, because the world is like a jungle, full of predators and danger. But when I enter it, I go forth in confidence, knowing that You are with me. In fact, Lord, I claim Your promise of protection every time I travel on foot, by car, by bus or plane by asking that Your protecting angels go with me.

Tribulation

God's Word to Me

In the world you will have tribulation; but be of good cheer, I have overcome the world.

John 16:33, NKJV

I am not asking you to take them out of the world, but I ask you to protect them from the evil one.

John 17:15, NRSV

Prayer-Meditation

Thank You, Lord, for Your realism. You have never promised to take us believers out of the world or that You would be an insurance policy against every kind of trouble. We are grateful for this sure promise of an overcoming victory in times of tribulation. We rest in the assurance that You have overcome the world.

True Happiness

God's Word to Me

He who loves money will not be satisfied with money; nor he who loves wealth, with gain: this also is vanity.

Ecclesiastes 5:10, RSV

Read James 5:5.

Prayer-Meditation

Father, You are helping me to see the pattern of evil that results from love of money, from greed, vanity, selfishness, lust, corruption. I not only see this about myself, but I am also deeply troubled about what I see in my nation. A "me-first" philosophy of unabashed selfishness and greed is masquerading under lofty, pretentious jargon about self-fulfillment.

Father, save us from the wreckage that such selfishness brings. Show us before it is too late that true joy and happiness come from a lifestyle that seeks to give, not receive, that seeks a spirit-to-Spirit bonding with You.

Prayer for Integrity

God's Word to Me

For to us a child is born, to us a son is given; and the government will be upon his shoulder.

Isaiah 9:6, RSV

Read Proverbs 29:2.

Prayer-Meditation

Lord Jesus, we ask You to guide the people of this nation as they exercise their dearly bought privilege of franchise. May it neither be ignored unthinkingly nor undertaken lightly. As citizens all over this land go to the ballot boxes ... we ask You to lead America in the paths where You would have her walk.

Peter Marshall

And for those of us who do not or cannot vote—may this be a day of special prayer for the election process. We ask that people of integrity come to office. We pray that they will love truth and prize our cherished freedoms.

Prayer for Officials

God's Word to Me

Of the increase of his govern-ment . . . there will be no end . . . to establish it, and to uphold it with justice and with righteous-ness from this time forth and for evermore.

Isaiah 9:7, RSV

Read 1 Kings 3:9.

Prayer-Meditation

Father-God, help those who have been elected to public office to understand the real source of their mandate—a mandate given by no party machine, received at no polling booth, but given by God; a man-date to govern wisely and well; a mandate to represent God at the heart of the nation; a man-date to do good in the Name of Him under whom this Republic was established.

Peter Marshall

And, Lord, as the newly elected ones prepare to take office, may they be imbued with a burning fire to serve You above all else.

Perseverance

God's Word to Me

And you will seek Me and find Me, when You search for Me with all your heart.

Jeremiah 29:13, NKJV

With my whole heart I have sought You; oh, let me not wan-der from Your commandments! Your word I have hidden in my heart, that I might not sin against You.

Psalm 119:10–11, NKJV

Read Luke 11:9–10.

Prayer-Meditation

Lord, You are indeed the Great Shepherd who will go to the most remote fields to find the lost sheep. But You are say-ing here that when we feel lost or have strayed and want to find You, then there is a time for per-severance on our part. I accept this, Lord. I pledge myself to seek You in every possible way.

Patience

God's Word to Me

Slowly, steadily, surely, the time approaches when the vision will be fulfilled. If it seems slow, do not despair, for these things will surely come to pass. Just be patient! They will not be overdue a single day!

Habakkuk 2:3, TLB

Let us not become weary in doing good, for at the proper time we will reap a harvest if we do not give up.

Galatians 6:9, NIV

Prayer-Meditation

How often, Lord, I have asked You to give me a vision of Your purpose and plan for my life. But true to my "let's have it now" generation, I tend to be impatient with Your majestic timing. Thank You for reminding me that in Your sovereign knowledge and power, You are never even a minute late. Give me the patience not to run ahead of You but to wait expectantly for Your Master Plan to unfold.

Self-Denial

God's Word to Me

Then Jesus said to His disciples, "If anyone desires to come after Me, let him deny himself, and take up his cross, and follow Me."

Matthew 16:24, NKJV

For they disciplined us for a short time as seemed best to them, but He disciplines us for our good, that we may share His holiness.

Hebrews 12:10, NASB

Prayer-Meditation

Our nature is to want more, not to deny ourselves. Your teaching here couldn't be plainer, Lord. I see so clearly that self-denial comes easier as we walk in obedience to You, as we learn to give ourselves away in service to others.

Jesus, we can learn from You how to carry our crosses. You bore Yours out of love for the Father and because You knew the glory it would accomplish.

203

The Servant Role

God's Word to Me

And whoever of you desires to be first shall be slave of all.

Mark 10:44, NKJV

After that, He poured water into a basin and began to wash the disciples' feet, and to wipe them with the towel with which He was girded.

John 13:5, NKJV

Prayer-Meditation

Lord, I have to make a confession here. To be a servant, to be submissive to another, to keep a servant's heart, goes against my grain. What I think You are saying here is that unless we learn the servant role in this life, we will have a most difficult time in the next, no matter how great our good works. Show me how to take the first step to becoming a good servant, Lord. Give me Your grace to bring this off.

Choices

God's Word to Me

You cannot drink the cup of the Lord and the cup of demons; you cannot partake of the Lord's table and of the table of demons.

1 Corinthians 10:21, NKJV

Again, the devil took him to a very high mountain and showed him all the kingdoms of the world and their splendor; and he said to him, "All these I will give you, if you will fall down and worship me."

Matthew 4:8–9, NRSV

Read Matthew 6:24.

Prayer-Meditation

The warning here is that life in this world is a series of choices. When God created us, He took a very big gamble—He gave us the freedom to accept Him or reject Him, not wanting to hold us puppet-like in a dance of life. Then He allowed Satan to set up a competing domain. I see all the choices, Lord. I choose to follow You whatever the cost.

For the Sorrowing

God's Word to Me

He [the Lord] has sent me to bind up the brokenhearted.

Isaiah 61:1, RSV

For His anger is but for a moment, His favor is for life; weeping may endure for a night, but joy comes in the morning.

Psalm 30:5, NKJV

Read Matthew 5:4 and Revelation 21:4.

Prayer-Meditation

You have suffered grief as we have, Lord, and have Yourself been broken. It eases our pain to have You share our plight—enter into it with us. You know how to comfort us with the right words, the right counsel to give us as You wrap our hearts with Your love.

I praise You that though our "weeping may endure for a night . . . joy comes in the morning" (Psalm 30:5).

To Bear Good Fruit

God's Word to Me

Every branch in Me that does not bear fruit He takes away; and every branch that bears fruit He prunes, that it may bear more fruit.

John 15:2, NKJV

The second son he named Ephraim and said, "It is because God has made me fruitful in the land of my suffering."

Genesis 41:52, NIV

Prayer-Meditation

The two trees were only a few feet apart, but they were separated by a fence because they had different owners. One tree was very straight, its branches heavy laden with beautiful big red apples. The other tree was scraggy, unkept, too weary to feed and hold its fruit. A pitiably few infested apples lay on the ground around it.

Lord, I see the difference. When the "pruning" hurts and I cry out, don't cease Your pruning, for I want to bear Your fruit.

Cost of Discipleship

God's Word to Me

Beloved, I beg you as sojourners and pilgrims, abstain from fleshly lusts which war against the soul.

1 Peter 2:11, NKJV

For we are a fragrance of Christ to God among those who are being saved and among those who are perishing; to the one an aroma from death to death, to the other an aroma from life to life. And who is adequate for these things?

2 Corinthians 2:15–16, NASB

Prayer-Meditation

Lord, You call us to a difficult moral standard. It sets us apart as "squares" or prudes in an ofttimes hostile and ridiculing world. Yet we trust Your teaching here, Lord, as one that will bring us good health, creativity, and inner peace. We renounce all the false and evil attitudes of a life outside of Christ, and choose to be ambassadors of His Kingdom here on earth, no matter the cost.

The Life of Victory

God's Word to Me

For Christ also suffered once for sins, the just for the unjust, that He might bring us to God, being put to death in the flesh but made alive by the Spirit.

1 Peter 3:18, NKJV

Therefore, since Christ suffered in his body, arm yourselves also with the same attitude, because he who has suffered in his body is done with sin.

1 Peter 4:1, NIV

Prayer-Meditation

Jesus has given us salvation and the Holy Spirit indwells us. But a life of victory and power can hinge on three things: an act, a purpose, and a habit.

Lord, by Your Holy Spirit maintain in me a continuing act of surrender to Your Lordship. Help me to keep a steady purpose in everything, willing to do as You would wish. Enable me to build a daily habit of being alone with You, my Bible open, my knees bent, and my spirit united with Yours.

Endurance

God's Word to Me

Strengthened with all might, according to His glorious power, for all patience and longsuffering with joy.

Colossians 1:11, NKJV

And not only that, but we also boast in our sufferings, knowing that suffering produces endurance, and endurance produces character, and character produces hope.

Romans 5:3–4, NRSV

Prayer-Meditation

From the lives of the apostles we learn that endurance was one of the chief credentials of God's "sent ones." To remain steadfast under continuous pressure was a test of their calling.

The situation has not changed. We who follow Jesus today find, as did the apostles, that spiritual power, along with joy and patience, is manifest as we learn to endure.

Lord, be my strength so that I will learn to endure joyously.

Overcoming Difficulties

God's Word to Me

Fear not . . . for I am with you; do not look around you in terror and be dismayed, for I am your God. I will strengthen and harden you [to difficulties]. . . . For I, the Lord your God, hold your right hand.

Isaiah 41:10, 13, AMP

Read John 16:7.

Prayer-Meditation

I begin to understand that Your way is not to remove my difficulties immediately but to give me a basis to cope with them through Your Word, through prayer and through my relying upon Your Spirit indwelling me. I also see that You would take from me self-pity, all "what-ifs," any wallowing in remorse, any thought of "what I deserve." Praise You, Father, for Your strong right hand holding me up.

Light Overcomes Darkness

God's Word to Me

The god of this world hath blinded the minds of them which believe not, lest the light of the glorious gospel of Christ, who is the image of God, should shine unto them.

2 Corinthians 4:4, KJV

In the same way, let your light shine before men, that they may see your good deeds and praise your Father in heaven.

Matthew 5:16, NIV

Prayer-Meditation

Jesus, You said that if we were to let our light shine, the darkness could not overcome it. I ask You now to so fill my life with Your Light that the darkness of disbelief will just disappear from the minds of those I meet. Show me, Lord, how to keep my light shining day after day, week after week, in every kind of situation.

Giving Up Control

God's Word to Me

And the serpent said to the woman, "You will not surely die. For God knows that in the day you eat of it your eyes will be opened, and you will be like God, knowing good and evil."

Genesis 3:4–5, NKJV

He was humble and walked the path of obedience all the way to death—his death on the cross.

Philippians 2:8, TEV

Prayer-Meditation

O Lord, this has been the bane of my life—wanting to be a "god," to have power over people. Your Word shows me it is the tempter working on me as he did on Eve. Deliver me from my adversary, Lord, that I may walk in love and peace with my fellowmen and not try to control them. Remove from me any desire to be a manipulator.

Worship

God's Word to Me

Now the glory of the Lord rested on Mount Sinai. . . . The sight of the glory of the Lord was like a consuming fire on the top of the mountain.

Exodus 24:16–17, NKJV

O worship the LORD in the beauty of holiness; tremble and reverently fear before Him, all the earth.

Psalm 96:9, AMP

Prayer-Meditation

Lord God Almighty, there are times when chatty familiarity with You is out of place, when all prayer seems inadequate, when we are rendered speechless as Your love and power overwhelm us.

God's Grace

God's Word to Me

For the grace of God that brings salvation has appeared to all men.

Titus 2:11, NKJV

The centurion replied, "Lord, I do not deserve to have you come under my roof. But just say the word, and my servant will be healed."

Matthew 8:8, NIV

Prayer-Meditation

Lord, I have been going through a period when I allow myself to think things like, "I deserve to spend some money on myself," or "I deserve to make this a 'be-good-to-me-day.'" I know this opens the door to Satan because I am reverting to the primary sin of the human race—my "right" to myself, and thus denying Your sacrifice on the cross.

Thank You for the truth that I deserve nothing from Your hands, and that every good gift comes to me by pure grace.

Rise Above Discouragement

God's Word to Me

Why are you cast down, O my soul? And why are you disquieted within me? Hope in God, for I shall yet praise Him for the help of His countenance.

Psalm 42:5, NKJV

Read Isaiah 61:3.

Prayer-Meditation

Some unknown saint has left us this pithy sentence: "All discouragement is from the devil."

One of Satan's prime devices is to trick us into sinning by "giving up" on God.

Lord, with the psalmist, I ask Your light on the *why* of my discouragement. Help me always to remember that despair and negativism are the opposite of hope and faith and a lie from the father of lies.

Mercy

God's Word to Me

And as you wish that men would do to you, do so to them.... And you will be sons of the Most High; for he is kind to the ungrateful and the selfish. Be merciful, even as your Father is merciful.

Luke 6:31, 35–36, RSV

Read Matthew 18:23–35.

Prayer-Meditation

Give us grace and strength to forebear and to persevere. Offenders, give us grace to accept and to forgive offenders. Forgetful ourselves, help us to bear cheerfully the forgetfulness of others.... Purge out of every heart the lurking grudge.

Robert Louis Stevenson

Lord, I see the lack of mercy in me. I pray that Your mercy will flow through me and out to those people whom You bring to my attention.

Jealousy

God's Word to Me

[Love] does not rejoice at wrong, but rejoices in the right.

1 Corinthians 13:6, RSV

And this commandment we have from Him: that he who loves God must love his brother also.

1 John 4:21, NKJV

Prayer-Meditation

Lord, these verses have been a sharp check for me. Are there people close to me, even family members, whom I would rather see fail than succeed? I confess there are, and I excuse this by saying, "Because of their wrong lifestyle they don't deserve success." Yet I see this as a lack of love, judgmentalism, even jealousy, and hand it over to You for forgiveness and cleansing.

The Giving Principle

God's Word to Me

All Mine are Yours, and Yours are Mine. . . . Give, and it will be given to you: good measure, pressed down, shaken together, and running over will be put into your bosom. For with the same measure that you use, it will be measured back to you.

John 17:10; Luke 6:38, NKJV

Read Proverbs 11:25.

Prayer-Meditation

I praise You, Father, for creating a world not only supplied with everything we need, but also aflame with beauty lavished everywhere. Enable me to grasp deep in my spirit that there is never lack in You, Lord, only love of beauty and opulent abundance; and that we set this abundance in motion only by giving.

What an amazing principle that as I give "pressed down and running over," what I need will be returned to me as surely as the tide must return to the shore.

Materialism

God's Word to Me

And the ones that fell among thorns are those who, when they have heard, go out and are choked with cares, riches, and pleasures of life, and bring no fruit to maturity.

Luke 8:14, NKJV

For all that is in the world, the lust of the flesh and the lust of the eyes and the boastful pride of life, is not from the Father, but is from the world.

1 John 2:16, NASB

Prayer-Meditation

Thank You, Lord, for showing me that affluence can be a trip to a sterile life. You have given me enough abundance to understand that the care of too many possessions can choke life by complicating it. Show me how to simplify my life on the basis of Your priorities, so that I can bring forth more fruit.

Being a Good Steward

God's Word to Me

He said to His disciples, "Gather up the fragments that remain, so that nothing is lost."

John 6:12, NKJV

Your plenty will supply what they need, so that in turn their plenty will supply what you need. . . . "He who gathered much did not have too much, and he who gathered little did not have too little."

2 Corinthians 8:14–15, NIV

Prayer-Meditation

Lord Jesus, this teaching says to me that even though our Father "owns all the cattle on a thousand hills," He wants nothing to be wasted. It must sicken You to see the extravagant misuse of food by a small portion of the world's population while the larger percentage are hungry and undernourished. Lord, I make this commitment to be ever grateful for Your meeting my needs, to be a responsible steward of what I have, and to be generous in giving to those who are in want or are less fortunate.

Thankfulness

God's Word to Me

When you reap the harvest of your land, do not reap to the very edges of your field or gather the gleanings of your harvest. Do not go over your vineyard a second time or pick up the grapes that have fallen. Leave them for the poor and the alien. I am the LORD your God.

Leviticus 19:9–10, NIV

When you beat your olive trees, do not strip what is left; it shall be for the alien, the orphan, and the widow.

Deuteronomy 24:20, NRSV

Prayer-Meditation

Father, from the days of the Pilgrims even unto now, You have dealt bountifully with us in this good land. Help us never to take this rain of blessings for granted, nor attribute it solely to *our* efforts.

So may we carry our gratitude into the grace of sharing. What lonely or needy ones would You have sit at our table? Lead us to them, Father.

The Holy Ten Percent

God's Word to Me

And all the tithe of the land, whether of the seed of the land or of the fruit of the tree, is the Lord's. It is holy to the Lord.

Leviticus 27:30, NKJV

Each of you must bring a gift in proportion to the way the LORD your God has blessed you.

Deuteronomy 16:17, NIV

Prayer-Meditation

Your word here is clear: ten percent of my income belongs to You. Before taxes. When I hang onto it, I am robbing You. This is a holy obligation, Lord.

Worship

God's Word to Me

Then David danced before the Lord with all his might.... David and all the house of Israel brought up the ark of the Lord with shouting and with the sound of the trumpet.

2 Samuel 6:14–15, NKJV

Let everything that has breath and every breath of life praise the Lord! Praise you the Lord!— Hallelujah!

Psalm 150:6, AMP

Prayer-Meditation

Lord, Your servant David was a master of praise and had immense variety in worship because he allowed the Spirit of God to direct it. Sometimes there was overflowing, uninhibited joy; at times, quietness— silence; at other times, reverence clothed in the towering words of the liturgy of the "Church Militant and Triumphant."

Lord, give us, too, the flexibility of Your Spirit in worship.

Deeper Truth

God's Word to Me

But solid food belongs to those who are of full age ... who ... have their senses exercised to discern both good and evil.

Hebrews 5:14, NKJV

Give me understanding, that I may observe Thy law, and keep it with all my heart.

Psalm 119:34, NASB

Prayer-Meditation

Lord, to seek the solid food and deeper truths of Your teaching, this next month I pledge myself to give one hour a day to Your Word. Stretch my mind to receive more knowledge, increase my understanding of Your Word about right and wrong, and cleanse my body so that it can be a temple for Your Spirit.

My Prayer Requests

God's Answers

December

The Lordship of Jesus

God's Word to Me

For God so loved the world that He gave His only begotten Son, that whoever believes in Him should not perish but have everlasting life.

John 3:16, NKJV

Immediately Jesus reached out his hand and caught him. "You of little faith," he said, "why did you doubt?"

Matthew 14:31, NIV

Prayer-Meditation

Lord Jesus, today I dwell on these verses of Scripture. And to begin I must ask myself: is there the tiniest question in my mind that You are the Son of Almighty God? I do not want my belief here to be a mere intellectual acceptance of the fact of Your divinity, but to affirm that a rock-solid relationship exists between us . . . that *You are the Master of my life.*

True Kingship

God's Word to Me

As the Lord hath been with [David] my lord the king. . . .

1 Kings 1:37, KJV

The LORD forbid that I should stretch out my hand against the LORD's anointed. But please, take now the spear and the jug of water that are by his head, and let us go.

1 Samuel 26:11, NKJV

Prayer-Meditation

David was every inch a king and leader: whether as a shepherd lad putting a lion or bear to flight; or bringing down the giant Goliath in the name of the Lord of hosts; or leading the mighty warriors of Saul. But when, as a fugitive from Saul, he suddenly came upon his pursuer asleep, David refused to strike the killing blow. This was the mark of true kingship, for he who cannot be merciful cannot be God's anointed one.

The Lord Jesus showed true kingship when He laid down His life that He might take it up again.

Priority Number One

God's Word to Me

Seek ye first the kingdom of God, and his righteousness; and all these things shall be added unto you.

Matthew 6:33, KJV

Fight the good fight of the faith; take hold of the eternal life, to which you were called and for which you made the good confession in the presence of many witnesses.

1 Timothy 6:12, NRSV

Prayer-Meditation

Here is a powerful spiritual principle for today—and a hard test of our faith. Can we believe that if Jesus is number one in our lives, everything else will fall into place? This doesn't mean there will be no problems, only that the Problem-solver is in our corner.

Private Treasure

God's Word to Me

Moreover, because I have set my affection on the house of my God, in addition to all I have prepared for the holy house, I have a private treasure of gold and silver which I give for the house of my God.

1 Chronicles 29:3, AMP

And He saw also a poor widow putting in two mites [copper coins]. And He said, Truly I say to you, this poor widow has put in more than all of them.

Luke 21:2–3, AMP

Prayer-Meditation

As I learn more and more what it means to be Your disciple, Jesus, it demands of me a total commitment of all things internal and external. You know there are possessions and securities to which I cling. I give You permission to take my will and change it so that I *want* to commit all things and all of myself to You.

Greed

God's Word to Me

But when the husbandmen saw him, they reasoned among themselves, saying, This is the heir: come, let us kill him, that the inheritance may be ours.

Luke 20:14, KJV

For the grace of God that brings salvation has appeared to all men. It teaches us to say "No" to ungodliness and worldly passions, and to live self-controlled, upright and godly lives in this present age.

Titus 2:11–12, NIV

Prayer-Meditation

Lord, at first I dismissed this passage in Luke as not applicable to me. After all, I am certainly not a murderer. Then I considered the greed of these husbandmen. Am I free of this sin? Not entirely. Lord, I give You permission to purge this vice inside me so that any inclination I have to grasp for things will be turned into generosity.

Protection

God's Word to Me

Put on the whole armor of God, that you may be able to stand against the wiles of the devil.

Ephesians 6:11, RSV

My shield is with God, who saves the upright in heart.

Psalm 7:10, NASB

Prayer-Meditation

The protection devices of the world are not enough to guarantee our safety, Lord. Teach me how Your armor protects me against the virulent forces of evil so that in case of attack I will be able to hold my ground firmly, safe in the knowledge that You are my strength and security.

Knowing God

God's Word to Me

He who has seen me has seen the Father.

John 14:9, RSV

I am the living bread which came down from heaven. If anyone eats of this bread, he will live forever; and the bread that I shall give is My flesh, which I shall give for the life of the world.

John 6:51, NKJV

Prayer-Meditation

God, pure Spirit, had a problem: how could He bridge the chasm between the Creator and the created? How could He show man what He is really like? God solved this problem in the incarnation. Jesus broke into history; He became one of us. If we want to know what the Father is like, we have but to look at Jesus.

Father, I thank You that the crystal stream of Jesus' life so clearly and perfectly mirrors You.

Temptation

God's Word to Me

He [Jesus] said unto them, Pray that ye enter not into temptation.

Luke 22:40, KJV

Read Genesis 3:1.

Prayer-Meditation

As Christians our desire is that God will be glorified by the fulfillment of His purpose in our lives. So our Father clearly defines for us the functional boundaries of our relationship with Him—just as He did with Adam and Eve. As we accept His loving directive, God and man live in harmony. But watch out when Satan drops a subtle, contrary point of view into our minds: "Ye shall not surely die, but ye shall be as gods." Denounce it quickly and decisively; renounce Satan and his lies.

Lord, I pray that You will be my watchguard and my deliverer from all temptations.

Fellowship with God

God's Word to Me

O God, You are my God; early will I seek You; my soul thirsts for You; my flesh longs for You in a dry and thirsty land.

Psalm 63:1, NKJV

Read John 15:4.

Prayer-Meditation

'Tis not to ask for gifts alone,
I kneel in prayer before His
    throne;
But, seeking fellowship divine,
I feel His love, and know it
    mine,
When I can pray.

I ought to pray, because my
    voice
Can make the Father's heart
    rejoice;
He loves His child, and He will
    meet,
And hold communication
    sweet,
With one who prays.

Mary Russell Olivant, 1852

Love One Another

God's Word to Me

Beloved, if God so loved us, we ought also to love one another.

1 John 4:11, KJV

Above all, keep fervent in your love for one another, because love covers a multitude of sins.

1 Peter 4:8, NASB

Prayer-Meditation

All praise to our redeeming
    Lord,
Who joins us by His grace,
And bids us, each to each
    restored,
Together seek His face.

He bids us build each other up;
And gathered into one,
To our high calling's glorious
    hope,
We hand in hand go on.

Charles Wesley, 1788

Lord, thank You for the reminder that there is opportunity given here for us to experience a foretaste of heaven as we work through difficult relationships and enter into Your reconciliation.

The Blood's Protection

God's Word to Me

. . . According to the foreknowledge of God the Father, through sanctification of the Spirit, unto obedience and sprinkling of the blood of Jesus Christ. . . .

1 Peter 1:2, KJV

He is to take some of the bull's blood and with his finger sprinkle it on the front of the atonement cover; then he shall sprinkle some of it with his finger seven times before the atonement cover.

Leviticus 16:14, NIV

Read Exodus 24:4–8; Hebrews 12:24.

Prayer-Meditation

As the priests sprinkled the blood of the sacrificial lamb on the altar and on the people, so You have sprinkled me with the blood of Jesus! How awesome! Yet I find a well of joy within, knowing, Father, that You will keep me under the protection of His shed blood as I walk in obedience with You.

Temptation

God's Word to Me

No temptation has overtaken you except such as is common to man; but God is faithful, who will not allow you to be tempted beyond what you are able, but with the temptation will also make the way of escape, that you may be able to bear it.

1 Corinthians 10:13, NKJV

Surely he will save you from the fowler's snare and from the deadly pestilence.

Psalm 91:3, NIV

Prayer-Meditation

Thank You, Lord, for this great promise: that You know me all through, even my limitations; that even this promise leaves me without the usual excuse, "I couldn't help it," and without the luxury of any self-pity.

Today make me alert to temptation, to Your strengthening to bear it, and to Your appointed way of escape.

Our Highest Affection

God's Word to Me

Set your affection on things above, not on things on the earth.

Colossians 3:2, KJV

And on the third day there was a wedding in Cana of Galilee, and the mother of Jesus was there; and Jesus also was invited, and His disciples, to the wedding.

John 2:1–2, NASB

Prayer-Meditation

Paul is not telling us to live in a state of super-spirituality, for that would be hypocrisy. Jesus loved the world of nature. He enjoyed working with His hands in the Nazareth carpentry shop; He looked for opportunities to play with children. But His highest affection was to His Father, and that is where ours is to be.

Lord, please help me set the desire of my heart, too, on Your Kingdom and Your righteousness.

Expressing His Compassion

God's Word to Me

Be kind to one another, tender-hearted. . . .

Ephesians 4:32, NKJV

Therefore comfort each other and edify one another, just as you also are doing.

1 Thessalonians 5:11, NKJV

Prayer-Meditation

Lord, when another person gets in my way or bothers me today, remind me to respond to him or her with Your tenderness and compassion. Today I will make that telephone call to _____, who needs my encouragement. I will also write that letter just to let _____ know that I care.

Winter

God's Word to Me

. . . And it was winter.

John 10:22, KJV

For he directs the snow, the showers, and storm to fall upon the earth.

Job 37:6, TLB

Prayer-Meditation

This morning the grand outside is covered with a fluffy white blanket; icicles hang from the eaves of the house. Even the fire hydrant wears a cocky white cap. I saw a cardinal, brilliant and red against the dazzling white.

Thank You, Father, for the change of seasons. Thank You for the changes in our lives that help us grow. Thank You for the testing of cold weather.

And bless all those this day who are cold and cheerless, and who sorely need help and encouragement.

Love One Another

God's Word to Me

Let us love one another, for love is of God; and everyone who loves is born of God and knows God.

1 John 4:7, NKJV

Every day they continued to meet together in the temple courts. They broke bread in their homes and ate together with glad and sincere hearts, praising God and enjoying the favor of all the people.

Acts 2:46–47, NIV

Prayer-Meditation

O Lord, for those precious and rich friendships which are rooted and grounded in You, I give You thanks. The richness of Your love discovered through these relationships gives special meaning as we approach this holiday season. Continue to be the binding force and origin of our love. Teach us how to avoid selfishness and possessiveness so that we can be free to be Your love for others.

Keeping the Promise

God's Word to Me

Again you have heard that it was said to those of old, "You shall not swear falsely, but shall perform your oaths to the Lord."

Matthew 5:33, NKJV

If someone makes a careless vow, no matter what it is about, he is guilty as soon as he realizes what he has done.

Leviticus 5:4, TEV

Prayer-Meditation

Lord Jesus, forgive me for the many times I have made promises to people to pray for them and have then forgotten to do so. Help me to remember that to make a promise is to give an oath as unto You, and that the obligation to fulfill it is clear and binding.

Receiving Forgiveness

God's Word to Me

Neither do I condemn thee: go, and sin no more.

John 8:11, KJV

If You, LORD, should mark iniquities, O Lord, who could stand? But there is forgiveness with You, that You may be feared.

Psalm 130:3–4, NKJV

Prayer-Meditation

Jesus never berates or belittles us. He deems as sin any deed that hampers or binds human personality—as "missing the mark" of His wonderful plan for our lives—and thus a waste of our great potential. The problem is that all our past sins, if unforgiven, are still in the present tense because they still are a part of us.

Lord, I thank You that I can go back in time right now, present to You my sins of years ago, and have them forgiven. How great it is to be free of these burdens!

To Forgive One Another

God's Word to Me

And forgive us our debts, as we forgive our debtors.

Matthew 6:12, KJV

Read Matthew 5:23–24.

Prayer-Meditation

It is a startling truth, Father, that You can forgive me my sins (which are so numerous) only to the extent that I am willing to forgive my fellow human beings.

But how great it is that the minute I, a prodigal, turn back to You in repentance, You come running down the road to meet me. And also, Father, I am learning that whenever I am willing for Christ's sake to go more than halfway to mend a quarrel, You rush joyously ahead of me to prepare the way. Thank You that this kind of reconciliation matters so much to You!

Redemption

God's Word to Me

And him who comes to Me I will most certainly not cast out—I will never, no never reject one of them who comes to Me.

John 6:37, AMP

For there is one God; there is also one mediator between God and humankind, Christ Jesus, himself human, who gave himself a ransom for all,—this was attested at the right time.

1 Timothy 2:5–6, NRSV

Prayer-Meditation

Lord, what a glorious word to remember always for myself and for others. What joy to know that there is no human life so sordid, no sin so terrible, no case so extreme that the blood of Your cross does not cover it, that Your love does not embrace it. O Savior, thank You for coming to earth to rescue us from ourselves.

Prayer for Discernment

God's Word to Me

For false christs and false prophets will rise and show signs and wonders to deceive, if possible, even the elect.

Mark 13:22, NKJV

Keep a close watch on all you do and think. Stay true to what is right and God will bless you and use you to help others.

1 Timothy 4:16, TLB

Prayer-Meditation

I pray for discernment, Lord, to know a false prophet when I see one. Keep me from impulsive judgments of spiritual leaders when I disagree with any of them. But sound the warning bells inside me when You want me either to confront one with Your truth or simply to walk away.

Forgiveness

God's Word to Me

... Forbearing one another and, if one has a complaint against another, forgiving each other; as the Lord has forgiven you, so you also must forgive.

Colossians 3:13, RSV

Read Genesis 50:18–19; Matthew 18:21–35.

Prayer-Meditation

Lord, as I consider forgiving _____, I confess there's a wrenching that goes on inside me. This action will cost me my sense of justice. My anger and resentment seem a proper retaliation for the wrong done me. And yet, Your command is there: to forgive. Therefore, in my will I *do* forgive, in spite of all my emotions shrieking to the contrary. I will hold onto this grudge no longer; I release it and ask You to help me wipe the slate clean.

Burning Heart

God's Word to Me

Did not our heart burn within us while He talked with us . . . ?

Luke 24:32, NKJV

I baptize you with water for repentance. But after me will come one who is more powerful than I, whose sandals I am not fit to carry. He will baptize you with the Holy Spirit and with fire.

Matthew 3:11, NIV

Prayer-Meditation

I am eager, Lord, to have the "burning heart" which the disciples experienced when Jesus reappeared to them. There is a secret here that entrances me. Lord Jesus, I believe You are ready to light a fire in any of us who will go all out with You. I volunteer right now.

Christmas Eve

God's Word to Me

And she gave birth to her first-born son and wrapped him in swaddling cloths, and laid him in a manger, because there was no place for them in the inn.

Luke 2:7, RSV

Listen! I am standing at the door, knocking; if you hear my voice and open the door, I will come in to you and eat with you, and you with me.

Revelation 3:20, NRSV

Prayer-Meditation

Those words "no place for them" prick my conscience this holiday season, Lord. I wonder how many people have no place to go this Christmas. Is there any lonely person I could invite to share my home, my food, my companionship?

Lord Jesus, I would find room in the inn of my heart for You this Christmastide by sharing my blessings with someone else.

Christmas Day

God's Word to Me

For there is born to you this day in the city of David a Savior, who is Christ the Lord. And this will be the sign to you: You will find a Babe wrapped in swaddling cloths, lying in a manger.

Luke 2:11–12, NKJV

And when they had come into the house, they saw the young Child with Mary His mother, and fell down and worshiped Him. And when they had opened their treasures, they presented gifts to Him: gold, frankincense, and myrrh.

Matthew 2:11, NKJV

Prayer-Meditation

Dear Lord, since Christ was born in a simple Bethlehem manger, I will celebrate today by acts of simplicity: a prayer of praise, partaking of the sacraments, a demonstration of love as I give gifts to others from my heart.

The Glory of Christmas

God's Word to Me

And the shepherds returned, glorifying and praising God for all the things that they had heard and seen, as it was told unto them.

Luke 2:20, KJV

Mary said, "My heart praises the Lord; my soul is glad because of God my Savior."

Luke 1:46–47, TEV

Prayer-Meditation

O Lord Jesus, we thank You for the joys of this season, for the divine love that was shed abroad among men when You first came as a little child. Help each one of us to keep Christmas alive in our hearts and in our homes, that it may continue to glow, to shed its warmth, to speak its message during all the bleak days of winter. So may Christmas linger with us, even as You, Lord, are beside us the whole year through.

Peter Marshall

Remembering His Blessing

God's Word to Me

Bless the Lord, O my soul; and all that is within me, bless His holy name! Bless the Lord, O my soul, and forget not all His benefits: Who forgives all your iniquities, Who heals all your diseases, Who redeems your life from destruction, Who crowns you with lovingkindness and tender mercies.

Psalm 103:1–4, NKJV

Read 1 Peter 1:8–9.

Prayer-Meditation

Lord, with such joyous reassurance as this, Your own Word to me, my praise rises like a fountain. As I let my mind roam back over this year, what stands out are Your mercies, the many answers to prayer, all crowned indeed with Your lovingkindness. Thank You, thank You!

Our Covenant God

God's Word to Me

For this is My blood of the new covenant. . . .

Matthew 26:28, AMP

Prayer-Meditation

And now, beloved, let us bind ourselves with willing bonds to our Covenant God, and take the yoke of Christ upon us.

This taking of His yoke . . . means that we are heartily content that He appoint us our place and work, and that He alone be our reward.

Christ has many services to be done; some are easy, others are difficult: some bring honour, others bring reproach; some are suitable to our natural inclination and temporal interests, others are contrary to both. In some we may please Christ and please ourselves, in others we cannot please Christ except by denying ourselves. Yet the power to do all these things is assuredly given us in Christ, who strengtheneth us.

And the Covenant which I have made on earth, let it be ratified in heaven.

John Wesley

The Communion of Saints

God's Word to Me

Therefore we also, since we are surrounded by so great a cloud of witnesses. . . .

Hebrews 12:1, NKJV

Prayer-Meditation

Let saints on earth unite to
    sing,
With those to glory gone;
For all the servants of our
    King,
In earth and heaven are one:

E'en now by faith we join our
    hands,
With those that went before,
And greet the blood-redeemed
    bands,
On the eternal shore.

Charles Wesley, 1788

What tremendous encouragement, Lord Jesus, to know that so many of Your followers have kept the faith and have become witnesses at home with You in the eternal household of faith. I look forward to joining You there.

Faith Triumphant

God's Word to Me

All flesh shall see the salvation of God.

Luke 3:6, KJV

For he [Abraham] was waiting expectantly and confidently, looking forward to the city which has fixed and firm foundations, whose Architect and Builder is God.

Hebrews 11:10, AMP

Prayer-Meditation

God of our Fathers and our God, give us the faith to believe in the ultimate triumph of righteousness. . . . We pray for the bifocals of faith—that see the despair and the need of the hour, but also see, farther on, the patience of our God working out His plan in the world.

Peter Marshall

The Gift of Faith

God's Word to Me

For by the grace . . . given to me
I warn every one among you not
to estimate and think of himself
more highly than he ought . . .
but to rate his ability . . . each
according to the degree of faith
apportioned by God to him.

Romans 12:3, AMP

Read Isaiah 12:2.

Prayer-Meditation

This morning Your Word tells
me that my rating in the Kingdom of God is not on the basis
of my good works but on the
degree of my faith (to what
extent I believe and trust You to
handle my life and the lives of
those I love). I am learning also
that in Your eyes, Lord, unbelief
is the greatest sin of all.

Therefore, very simply, Lord,
I ask You for the gift of faith—
the capacity, the ability, and the
stamina—to trust You for anything the new year holds. Thank
You that this greatest gift of faith
is Yours to bestow.

My Prayer Requests

_____
_____
_____
_____
_____
_____
_____
_____
_____
_____

God's Answers

_____
_____
_____
_____
_____
_____
_____
_____
_____
_____

Topical Index

Abiding in the Light   Jul. 2
Abortion   May 14
Adoration   May 15
Adoration   May 22
Adultery   Aug. 17
Adventurous Living   May 2
Adventurous Prayer   Mar. 16
Asking Prayer   Mar. 12
Atonement   Sep. 11
Authority of Jesus, The   Sep. 19

Being a Good Steward   Nov. 26
Being Super-Spiritual   Jul. 15
Blocks to Answered Prayer   Sep. 10
Blocks to Prayer   Jan. 17
Blood's Protection, The   Dec. 11
Boldness   Sep. 8
Bread of Life   Apr. 29
Burning Heart   Dec. 23

Caring for Others   Sep. 28
Caring Shepherd, The   Aug. 2
Challenge to Children   May 10
Challenge to Parents   May 9
Choices   Nov. 10
Christian Character   Sep. 24
Christian Growth   Mar. 5
Christmas Day   Dec. 25
Christmas Eve   Dec. 24
Christ's Humanity   Mar. 1
Christ's Humanity   Jun. 18
Christ's Humanity   Aug. 7
Christ's Humanity   Oct. 8
Christ's Humanity   Oct. 16
Christ's Passion   Mar. 29
Christ's Prayer for His People   Mar. 27

Christ's Sacrifice   Mar. 30
Cleansing of the Heart   Jan. 2
Cleansing of the Heart   Oct. 17
Cleanse My Thoughts   Apr. 23
Commitment   Jul. 29
Commitment   Sep. 13
Communion of Saints, The   Dec. 29
Constant Prayer   Mar. 9
Conversation with God   May 5
Cost of Discipleship   Nov. 13
Courage to Fight Evil   Sep. 16
Covetousness   Aug. 20
Criticism   May 21
Crowd Pressure   Apr. 4
Cry of the Human Heart   Feb. 10

Deeper Truth   Nov. 30
Dependence upon God   Jul. 25
Depression   Jan. 20
Destructive Tongue   Aug. 27
Disciplining the Tongue   Jul. 17
Dreams and Visions   Jan. 30

Endurance   Nov. 15
Empty Self, The   Sep. 3
Expressing His Compassion   Dec. 14

Facing Adversity   Jul. 27
Faith   Feb. 5
Faith   Feb. 6
Faith   Feb. 7
Faith   Feb. 8
Faith   Feb. 22
Faith   Jul. 8
Faith   Sep. 21
Faithfulness   Apr. 7

Faith Triumphant   Dec. 30
False Leadership   Sep. 20
False Peace   Jul. 6
False Prophets   Jun. 29
False Prophets   Sep. 22
False Witness   Aug. 19
Fear of the Lord   Jul. 14
Fearing God   Oct. 1
Fellowship with God   Dec. 9
Forgive   Aug. 24
Forgiveness   Dec. 22
Forgiveness of Sin   Sep. 7
For Parents   Jun. 14
For the Sorrowing   Nov. 11
For the Troubled   Feb. 4
Freedom and Authority   Feb. 24
Freedom from Tyranny   Jul. 3
Freedom in Jesus   Jan. 24
Freedom to Choose   Sep. 18
Fret Not   Jun. 16
Friendship with God   Jun. 9
Fullness of Joy, The   Aug. 31

Gathering the Harvest   Oct. 10
Gethsemane   Apr. 3
Gift of Faith, The   Dec. 31
Gift of Grace, The   Oct. 26
Giving Correction   Sep. 15
Giving in Secret   Sep. 9
Giving Principle, The   Nov. 24
Giving Up Control   Nov. 18
Glory of Christmas, The   Dec. 26
God as Spirit   May 29
God Is with You   Nov. 1
God's Call   Apr. 26
God's Grace   Nov. 20
God's Guidance   Feb. 23
God's Guidance   Jul. 9
God's Love   Feb. 19
God's Rest   Apr. 24
God the Matchmaker   May 12
Gossip   Jul. 18
Gossiping Tongues   Sep. 6
Greed   Dec. 5
Grievous Words   Aug. 23

Healing Power   Oct. 11
Healing Word, The   Oct. 12
Hearing God's Voice   Jan. 8

Heart Attitude   Jun. 6
Heart Examination   Oct. 4
Heart's Home, The   Jan. 1
He Finishes His Work   Mar. 26
Help in Trouble   Oct. 30
High Road, The   Jul. 12
His Forgiveness   Feb. 25
His Presence Satisfies   Jan. 29
Holy Ten Percent, The   Nov. 28
Honor Thy Parents   Aug. 15
Hospitality   Oct. 19
Humanity of Jesus, The   Mar. 28

Idolatry   Oct. 5
In Everyday Life   Sep. 2
In His Presence   Jul. 23
Inner Beauty   Aug. 30
Intercession   Mar. 8
Intercession for Believers   May 28

Jealousy   Nov. 23
Jesus Our Advocate   Jun. 2
Jesus, Our Paschal Sacrifice   Apr. 2
Jesus' Prayer for Us   Oct. 31
Jesus, The Answer   Jan. 21
Jesus, the Glorified Lord   Jun. 3
Jesus, the Intercessor   Mar. 15
Joy   Jan. 13
Joy   Apr. 8
Joy   Apr. 25
Joy   Jun. 23
Joy of Work, The   Sep. 1
Joyous Expectancy   May 1

Keeping Power   Feb. 26
Keeping the Promise   Dec. 17
Keeping the Sabbath   Aug. 14
Knowing God   Oct. 3
Knowing God   Dec. 7

Let God Do It   Oct. 23
Life of Victory, The   Nov. 14
Lifting Burdens   May 25
Light and Darkness   Aug. 21
Light Overcomes Darkness   Sep. 17
Light Overcomes Darkness   Nov. 17
Listening Heart, A   May 4
Listening Heart, The   Feb. 11
Listening Heart, The   Mar. 31

Living in the Present   Feb. 16
Living Sacrifice   Jul. 31
Living Word, The   Oct. 6
Loneliness   Mar. 3
Loneliness   May 3
Lord's Name, The   Aug. 13
Lordship of Jesus, The   Dec. 1
Love   Jan. 11
Love   Feb. 12
Love   Apr. 27
Love   May 31
Love of Honesty   Jun. 27
Love of Righteousness   Jun. 25
Love of Truth   Jun. 26
Love One Another   Jan. 28
Love One Another   Dec. 10
Love One Another   Dec. 16
Love That Endures   Jun. 10
Love That Lasts   Apr. 30
Love Your Neighbor   Jun. 11
Loving God   Oct. 2
Loving the Unlovely   Aug. 22

Marriage Vow   Jun. 13
Materialism   Nov. 25
Mercy   Feb. 17
Mercy   Nov. 22
Mind Renewal   Aug. 10
Ministering Angels   Jul. 30
Ministering Angels   Sep. 29
Money in Perspective   Sep. 5
Mother, I Love You   May 11
Moving the Hard Heart   Jun. 7
Mountain-Moving Prayer   Sep. 26
My Secret Place   Sep. 30

Nature of God, The   Jan. 3
Nature of God, The   Jan. 4
Nature of God, The   Jan. 5
Nature of God, The   Jan. 6
Nature of God, The   Feb. 2
Never Lose Hope   Oct. 18
New Creature, The   Jun. 1
New Direction   May 17
New Life, The   Jan. 31
New Life   Apr. 22
No Graven Image   Aug. 12
No Other Gods   Aug. 11
Not to Kill   Aug. 16

Obedience   Jan. 7
Obedience   Apr. 18
Obedience   May 24
Obedience   Jul. 7
Obedience   Oct. 29
Obedient Children   Feb. 15
Open My Ears   Jan. 12
Opportunity   Aug. 28
Our Bulwark against Temptation
      Aug. 9
Our Covenant God   Dec. 28
Our Earthly Treasures   Jul. 21
Our Highest Affection   Dec. 13
Our Unchanging God   Oct. 27
Overcoming Difficulties   Nov. 16
Overcoming Discouragement   Sep. 27
Overcoming Trouble   May 26

Patience   Jan. 22
Patience   Feb. 13
Patience   Nov. 7
Peacemakers, The   Aug. 26
Persecution   Apr. 11
Perseverance   Nov. 6
Persistent Prayer   May 13
Persistence in Prayer   Sep. 25
Pleasing Jesus   Jan. 23
Positive Prayer   Jan. 16
Poverty   Jun. 15
Power of Agreement, The   May 20
Power of His Name, The   Oct. 20
Practicing His Presence   Mar. 22
Praise   Mar. 17
Praise   May 7
Praise   Oct. 21
Praising God   Feb. 20
Praising Others   Jun. 30
Prayer for Discernment   Dec. 21
Prayer for Children   Jun. 19
Prayer for Integrity   Nov. 4
Prayer for Nations   Jul. 5
Prayer for New Believers   Feb. 27
Prayer for Officials   Nov. 5
Prayer for a Sinner   May 30
Prayer for Small Needs   Mar. 7
Prayer for Strength   Jul. 20
Prayer in Secret   Jan. 18
Prayer That Upholds, The   Oct. 22
Prayer without Ceasing   Jan. 19

Praying Parents   Feb. 14
Priority in Prayer   Jan. 15
Priority Number One   Dec. 3
Private Treasure   Dec. 4
Protection   Mar. 2
Protection   Mar. 11
Protection   Apr. 20
Protection   Jun. 20
Protection   Jun. 21
Protection   Jun. 22
Protection   Sep. 14
Protection   Dec. 6
Purity   Mar. 23
Pursue Peace   Jun. 4

Quietness of His Presence, The   Jul. 24

Reality of His Presence, The   Oct. 28
Receiving Forgiveness   Dec. 18
Redemption   Mar. 14
Redemption   Dec. 20
Rejoice   Oct. 25
Rejoicing   Apr. 13
Release for the Captive   Aug. 5
Relinquishment   Oct. 24
Remembering His Blessing   Dec. 27
Renewal Time   Apr. 9
Repentance   Mar. 18
Repentance   Sep. 12
Repentance for Our Nation   Jul. 4
Resurrection, The   Apr. 6
Resurrection Appearances   Apr. 12
Resurrection of Hope   Apr. 10
Resurrection Promise   Apr. 14
Rise Above Discouragement   Nov. 21

Sacrifice of Prayer, The   Jun. 17
Security   May 18
Seeking Wholeness   Jun. 12
Self-Deception   Oct. 13
Self-Denial   Nov. 8
Selflessness   May 6
Servant Role, The   Jun. 28
Servant Role, The   Nov. 9
Serving God   Jul. 16
Sharing the Good News   Mar. 4
Sharing the Good News   Oct. 7
Sharing the Good News   Oct. 9
Sonship   Jul. 22

Sovereignty of God, The   Apr. 1
Spirit-Led Bible Reading   Aug. 29
Spiritual Cleansing   Mar. 20
Spiritual Food   Aug. 8
Spiritual Treasure   Sep. 4
Spiritual Vision   Feb. 1
Spiritual Warfare   Feb. 9
Spiritual Warfare   Mar. 24
Spiritual Warfare   Apr. 21
Spiritual Warfare   May 19
Spiritual Warfare   Aug. 3
Stealing   Aug. 18
Surrender of the Will   Mar. 19

Temptation   Jan. 25
Temptation   Jan. 26
Temptation   Jan. 27
Temptation   May 23
Temptation   Dec. 8
Temptation   Dec. 12
Thankfulness   Nov. 27
Thoughtless Words   Oct. 15
Time for Silence, A   Mar. 21
Time to Listen, A   Jul. 11
Tithing   Jan. 14
To Bear Good Fruit   Nov. 12
To Forgive One Another   Dec. 19
To Love My Neighbor   Aug. 25
Tongue, The   Mar. 6
Transfiguration, The   Apr. 16
Trial by Fire   Jul. 28
Tribulation   Nov. 2
True Happiness   Nov. 3
True Kingship   Dec. 2
Trust   Feb. 28
Trust   Apr. 5
Trust   Jul. 13
Trust for Tomorrow   May 8
Truth and Error   Sep. 23
Truth through His Word   Apr. 28
Turning Darkness to Light   Jul. 10
Two Who Agree   Oct. 14

Ultimate Truth   Aug. 1

Vision   Jul. 19
Vitality   Mar. 10

Waiting   Jun. 24

Walk in the Spirit   Jun. 5
Way Out of the Wilderness, The   Aug. 6
When in a Storm   Jul. 26
Wilderness Experience   May 16
Winning One Person   Jun. 8
Winter   Dec. 15
Winter of the Spirit   Feb. 3
Witnessing   Feb. 18
Witnessing   May 27
Witnessing   Jul. 1
Word, The   Jan. 9

Word, The   Jan. 10
Word, The   Feb. 21
Word, The   Mar. 25
Words of Faith   Mar. 13
Worship   Apr. 19
Worship   Aug. 4
Worship   Nov. 19
Worship   Nov. 29

Your Reservation with Jesus   Apr. 15